B. F. SKINNER

DR. RICHARD I. EVANS is Professor of Psychology and coordinates the graduate social psychology program at the University of Houston. He received his B.S. and M.S. degrees in Psychology at the University of Pittsburgh and his Ph.D. in Psychology at Michigan State University. Under a National Science Foundation grant, he has filmed dialogues with the world's most notable psychologists, including Carl Jung, Erich Fromm, Erik Erikson, and B. F. Skinner, from which the books in this series are derived. He is a pioneer in educational television and the social psychology of communication, and taught the nation's first college course on noncommercial television. His continuing concern with sound public education in psychology has led to frequent appearances on commercial and educational television programs. He has published a number of professional articles in social psychology. His most recent book is *Resistance to Innovation in Higher Education* (with Peter Leppmann).

B. F. SKINNER

RICHARD I. EVANS

The Man and His Ideas

E. P. DUTTON & CO., INC.
NEW YORK   1968

First Edition

To
my lovely wife
and children

Acknowledgments

In the long process involved in filming and taping the dialogues with B. F. Skinner and transcribing, editing, and integrating them into the present volume, I am indebted to a great many individuals. Though space prohibits mentioning everyone who so kindly assisted in this venture, I wish to express my appreciation to at least some of these individuals.

The skill and imagination of psychology graduate student Judith Woodard is significantly reflected in this volume, and for her efforts during the early stages of preparation of this volume I am most grateful.

Thanks are also due to psychology graduate student Peter Leppmann for his assistance in the final editing of the manuscript, which in particular included the integration of Skinner's reactions to the first draft, and the important details connected with developing and checking out the bibliography.

Grateful acknowledgment is made to the University of Houston for permission to utilize the printed texts of the filmed and taped dialogue. Mr. James Bauer, of the University of Houston, who functioned in the demanding role of technical director for the taping and filming sessions, should also be mentioned among those who have greatly assisted me.

At several points in the project we were fortunate to have the services of two able secretaries. In this respect I wish to express my thanks to Mrs. Carolyn Ramirez for her preliminary work on the manuscript and to Mrs. Peggy Leppmann, who with great patience and care handled the demanding chore of preparing the final form of the manuscript.

I am grateful for the support from the National Science Foundation, without which this project could not have been implemented.

Finally, the wonderful cooperation of Professor B. F. Skinner cannot be emphasized enough. Not only was he willing to participate in the filming and taping sessions that are involved in this project, but in spite of his extremely busy schedule, he was willing to edit and even in some instances amend the text of the material in printed form, so that this volume would not suffer in the transition from film and sound to print.

RICHARD I. EVANS
Professor of Psychology
University of Houston

CONTENTS

Preface

A recent survey based on a sampling of the membership of the American Psychological Association rated Dr. B. F. Skinner as perhaps the most influential contemporary psychologist. Dr. Skinner's contributions to research methodology in psychology include a powerful, precise refinement, which he calls "operant conditioning," of Pavlov's old concept of classical conditioning. His concern for what he believes to be the inadequacy of our formal educational system led to applying the principles of operant conditioning to a learning system which he calls the "teaching machine."

But Skinner's approach is concerned with more than merely methods and techniques. He challenges the very foundations of the means by which man in our society is shaped and controlled. He feels that too often man is forced to operate in an aversive system. This aversive system of control frequently involves threat of the consequences of failure. Skinner feels that this type of negative rein-

forcement in the long run is both inefficient and in-
effective. He believes that society must shift to a
system which emphasizes positive rather than negative reinforcement. This he feels will lead to development of man to his maximum capability and to a
good life.

The fact that he has developed techniques of
shaping behavior through a program of scheduled
reinforcement poses a threat to individuals with
humanistic values, who fear that Skinner's powerful
techniques of control will tend to dehumanize the
individual. To the readers who are concerned with
this possibility Skinner is given an opportunity in this
book to clarify his position and challenge the validity
of this criticism.

One can observe how Skinner feels *today* about
many of the ideas presented in his earlier works.
Furthermore, certain new ideas and areas of focus are
suggested that he plans to develop in forthcoming
books. But most of all, I would hope that through this
dialogue the reader will be left with a view of Skinner's orientation which suggests the difference between his "clean" system of behavior analysis, which
makes the fewest possible assumptions about the
"inner workings" of the organism, and the consider-
ably more involved systems of personality theory such
as psychoanalysis, which are almost exclusively concerned with the "inner workings" of the individual.

The reader who is relatively unacquainted with
Skinner's work will find here an introduction to his
contributions to psychology, while the reader who has
previously read a considerable amount of Skinner's

work should also find much of interest in this material.

A little of Dr. Skinner's background and present activity may be of interest. After completing his Ph.D. degree in psychology at Harvard University, he spent five years in basic research, for two years under a National Research Council fellowship and three as a Junior Fellow in the Harvard Society of Fellows. He then embarked on a highly productive research and teaching career that included posts at the University of Minnesota and Indiana University, before returning in 1948 to Harvard, where he is currently Edgar Pierce Professor of Psychology. To the student of the behavioral sciences he is known for the classic *The Behavior of Organisms* published in 1938, and such works as *Science and Human Behavior* (The Macmillan Company, 1953), *Verbal Behavior* (Appleton-Century-Crofts, 1957), *Cumulative Record* (Appleton-Century-Crofts, 1959), and *Schedules of Reinforcement* (Appleton-Century-Crofts, 1957) which he co-authored with C. B. Ferster. Although his research career in psychology was at first largely confined to the laboratory, he has since devoted much effort toward increasing our capability for coping with many crucial problems of mankind. His teaching machine has proved to be one of the most formidable innovations in the recent history of education. The concept of programmed instruction, which he originated, and the extension of operant conditioning to classroom management are the subjects of *The Technology of Teaching* (Appleton-Century-Crofts, 1968). His novel, *Walden Two* (The Macmillan Company, 1948), has perhaps more than anything else brought his ideas to the attention of society at large. His attempt in this novel to fashion a utopian society based on a planned order that would feature the elimination of aversive controls has provoked much discussion and controversy. *Walden Two* has been regarded as a most ingenious means of communicating to society Dr. Skinner's conception of a maximally effective society predicated on his crucial experiments in modifying behavior in an increasingly more productive direction.

This volume is the fourth in a series that is based on edited and amended transcripts of 16 mm. sound films and additional audio-taped discussions. *Conversations with Carl Jung and Reactions from Ernest Jones* (6), *Dialogue with Erich Fromm* (9), and *Dialogue with Erik Erikson* (10) were the preceding books in this series. Projected books will be based on dialogues with such noted contributors to personality psychology as Gordon Allport, Henry Murray, Gardner Murphy, Raymond Cattell, Ernest Hilgard, and Nevitt Sanford. Also in this series is a dialogue with playwright Arthur Miller from a psychological perspective.

This inclusion of Dr. Skinner in a series which features primarily personality psychologists is suggested by the fact that his approach to the analysis of behavior may be the most significant alternative to a personality psychology.

REACTIONS TO VARIOUS PSYCHOLOGICAL CONCEPTS

CHAPTER 1

Overview | Although Skinner's point of view is far different from that of Sigmund Freud, I felt the reader should have an opportunity to see how Skinner feels about some of Freud's basic views. Of particular interest here is Skinner's reaction to Freud's distinction between the conscious and the unconscious.

Other areas of continuing focus in psychology are the conceptions of motivation and emotions. In efforts to understand personality, most psychologists—including Freud—asked the question, *"Why* does the organism do what it does?" The answer that is given by psychologists is in terms of the individual's motives, ranging from hunger to the need for social approval. Motivation is defined as all conditions that arouse, direct, and sustain the organism. But to Skinner this traditional importance afforded motivation may be unnecessary. The study of emotions, of such concern to many psychologists, is also unimportant in Professor Skinner's scheme.

In present-day psychology, another area that has been of extreme interest has been how underlying physiological processes relate to psychological processes in the individual. Skinner criticizes the model which postulates this relationship.

Still another traditional area of interest in psychology has been the study of man's experience, how he views his world. The physical environment supplies certain stimuli or impulses, which in turn are reacted to by sense organs, and then are transmitted to the brain or "inside the head" of the individual. Many psychologists today have become more concerned with the process of perception, or how the person views the world from the inside out, than with the physical stimuli which trigger off perception. In this chapter Professor Skinner indicates his feeling that this process is not the most profitable focus for the student of behavior, explaining why he feels this way.

The basic model of conditioning of the organism was developed by the great Russian physiologist Ivan Pavlov. Systematic work on conditioning since Pavlov has provided much of the basis for the behavioristic view of man. Even in Professor Skinner's far from traditional kind of behaviorism, conditioning is a central component. Professor Skinner here reveals how he feels Pavlov's theory of the conditioned reflex affected his thinking. Skinner has developed an alternative model which he prefers to call "operant conditioning." Since this is perhaps one of the classic and unique facets of Skinner's contribution, the reader's attention is called to Skinner's own description of operant conditioning.

EVANS: Dr. Skinner, we might begin by getting your reactions to some of the other views in psychology which seem to have left some impact. For example, many individuals are introduced to psychology by an examination of the ideas of the founder of psychoanalysis, Sigmund Freud. What do you believe Freud was trying to say about the development of the individual, and how do you feel about these ideas? I know that you have discussed this extensively in an earlier publication of yours (45).

SKINNER: The Freudian mental apparatus doesn't make much sense to me. Freud made some very important contributions. As a determinist, he convinced many people that things formerly believed to be accidental were really lawful, and I think he was right on that point. But in filling in the gap between the events which he saw to be causally related, he chose to construct or piece together an elaborate system of mental events going on inside the organism. This was particularly true when he tried

to relate the behavior of the adult to what had happened to him as a child. Perhaps fifty years elapse during which no evidence of a causal effect is evident;
then suddenly something happens which looks as if it
were related to an event that happened to the individual as a child. Now, I believe that there are
connections of that kind, but the Freudian formulation doesn't very well represent what happened,
nor does it permit one to trace it to current behavior. A child is influenced and changed as a
biological entity by things that happen to him, but
the notion that somehow or other the child of our
past is still contained within us is a form of animism which serves no useful purpose in explaining
present behavior. Using the notion of sibling rivalry
for an example, suppose that an adult finds it im-
possible to be open and free in dealing with people
because of anxiety generated by punishment from his
father when he, as a child, struck his brother or sister.
You could say that the product of this early experience
has been converted into some sort of felt anxiety ex-
perienced at the present moment and that the present
behavioral disturbance is due to the felt anxiety. The
mental event is supposed to tie together the terminal
events, but it doesn't represent them properly. Re-
pressed wishes and fears are not a useful way of repre-
senting what happens to a person as a child, and I
don't feel the need for that kind of thing to explain
what's going on in the adult. I would say that Freud
did demonstrate important causal relations between
current behavior and things which happen to a person,
particularly in early childhood. But I don't believe

that he devised a useful conceptual system to connect the two.

EVANS: Yet Erich Fromm (9) emphasizes that the Freudians use an empirical approach which I suspect they *would* consider useful. There seems to be an important question of definition here. I note that you often use the term "empirical." You obviously mean something quite different from what the psychoanalysts do. I gather that what they think they "observe" in causal linkages is quite different from what you would describe as genuinely observable events.

SKINNER: Yes, there is a great deal to be said against stating causal linkages in terms of feelings, emotions, recollections, memories, and what not. My interest is in a science of behavior which is part of biology; it deals with observable events, not with the fictitious or metaphorical apparatus which Freudians feel they observe in the organism. So far as I'm concerned, these are versions of some sort of primitive animism.

EVANS: Freud's theory makes an important distinction between the conscious and unconscious. How do you feel about this?

SKINNER: It doesn't make any difference to me whether things are conscious or unconscious; the causality in behavior does not depend upon awareness. Awareness is something imposed upon us—we become aware of what we are doing and why we are doing it because society insists that we talk about these things. Society says, "Why are you doing that?" or "What are you going to do next?" and the child learns to look around and find something to talk about in reply. In that way he becomes a self-conscious person. The curious thing is that it is society that makes the individual observe himself—he has no reason to do so otherwise. There is nothing in a nonsocial environment which would ever generate awareness. Awareness is a reaction to a part of the environment— like any other behavior—but it happens to be a part of the environment contained within the organism itself.

EVANS: As we look further at Freud's theory of motivation, aside from his emphasis on the unconscious, we see that his theory—like most present-day theories—leaned heavily on the physiological notion of homeostasis, or balance. In these theories, motivation involves all of the conditions which arouse, direct, and sustain the organism. How do you feel about this approach to dealing with motivation from the *behavioral* standpoint?

SKINNER: There seem to be two issues here. One concerns the dimensions of behavior itself. I would define behavior as the movement of an organism in space with respect to itself or any other useful frame of reference. We sometimes deal with the products of movement, as in the case of speech, where we don't really observe muscular patterns. This is a pretty specific way to define behavior, and most people fall back on a more general description, using terms such as "adjustment," "adaptation," "homeostatic development," and so on. These are ways of avoiding an explicit description of behavior, and dangerous for that reason. However, if you are simply trying to account for the fact that one individual stays in balance while another does not, you can get along with a different frame of reference. In saying that a person copes with his situation successfully or that his condition improves over a period of time, you're not specifying any action. On the other hand, to identify the variables which lead an organism to adjust, you must be more specific about the behavior and its causes. It isn't enough to say, "Oh, there's a totality of conditions within the organism which bring about behavior." If you want to identify manipulable causes, you must isolate them and then test yourself by manipulating them and observing what happens. I would prefer to deal with the probability that a response will be emitted, but since it is not possible to deal with probability as such, I watch the rate with which a response is made. I would like to identify that rate as a function of manipulable, demonstrable conditions. If the response rate is not manipulable, if the response is not identifiable, you are helpless. You can guess, of course. The field of motivation, however, is not a very difficult one. If you have a situation in which you can observe the frequency with which an animal or a man engages in a given activity, then you can search for all the variables of which that frequency is a function. And when you've found them, then you can give a complete account of it.

EVANS: As a somewhat different approach to motivation, your colleague, Professor H. A. Murray (32), has enumerated specific needs of the individual. Another colleague, Professor D. C. McClelland (26), in studying one of these needs—achievement—suggests that the degree of early independence training to which the child is subjected will be directly related to the strength of his subsequent need for achievement. How do you feel about postulating various needs and determining early patterns in the child's life as a means of explaining their relative strength in the later life of the individual?

SKINNER: I don't see any reason to postulate a need anywhere along the line. People often complain that in our experimental work we use specific biological reinforcers—such as those related to hunger, thirst, or sex—and then they ask how we deal with nonbiological reinforcers which don't appear to reduce needs. But food is not reinforcing because it reduces a need. Eating changes a biological condition, but food is not reinforcing because it does so. As far as I'm concerned, if a baby is reinforced by the sound made by a rattle, the sound is just as useful as a reinforcer in accounting for behavior as food in the baby's mouth. That kind of distinction doesn't worry me. As to achievement, however, people generally tend to overlook the extraordinary importance of the conditions of reinforcement. The important thing is not that you are getting something; it is what you are doing at the moment you get it. I could make a pigeon a high achiever by reinforcing it on a proper schedule. I can't do it by ordering the needs. I don't know how to order needs. There is no way in which you can put a key in a slot and twist a need. What you can do is make an individual hungrier or you can use food skillfully as a reinforcer so that he will work at a very high rate when scarcely hungry at all. If you want people to be productive and active in various ways, the important thing is to analyze the contingencies of reinforcement, not the needs to be satisfied.

EVANS: To continue our discussion of motivation in psychology, do you feel that there is any more usefulness for the concept of *emotions* than for the concept of *needs*?

SKINNER: Not very much. An emotion is like a need, if it refers to an internal state which is supposed to account for behavior. You can no doubt find physiological processes which are related to specific, current, internal activities in an emotion as in food deprivation. It may be highly reinforcing to a person who is angry to damage someone verbally or physically, but to define anger as a particular pattern of autonomic responses existing at such a time will never succeed because these responses are common to a lot of other things, including many which we don't call emotions at all. Internal conditions after violent exercise would look awfully emotional if you recorded them on a polygraph, but they are not necessarily related to any emotion. Emotion, so far as I am concerned, is a matter of the probability of engaging in certain kinds of behavior defined by certain kinds of consequences. Anger is a heightened probability of attack, fear is a heightened probability of running away, and love is a heightened probability of positively reinforcing a loved person. Two people in love are continually reinforcing each other, and the mutual effect can be very powerful; it is an important factor in the analysis of human behavior. Physiology will no doubt be more meaningful when it can clarify these various aspects of the organism. At the moment its attempts to explain behavior are vague, and do not seem to me very useful.

EVANS: Do you think that, as a model at least, the

notion of physiological changes accompanying emotions might be valuable to the biologist interested in studying stress, even though it may not be relevant to the analysis of behavior?

SKINNER: I can imagine that it would. Someday all that is going on inside the organism will be understood, and its bearing on the responses of the organism to its environment will then be clear. As an analyst of behavior, I want to relate the probability of response to a large number of independent variables, even when these variables are separated in time and space. Something must fill in the gap, and I look forward to the time when physiologists will have something to say about it. But I have always objected to filling in the gap with speculative theories about what is going on inside. The physiologists should directly observe what they are talking about, and they are beginning to do that. It's a promising and hopeful sign. But most of the people who are active in exploring the mediators of behavior seem to be unaware of progress in the analysis of behavior. They are trying to explain fictional explanations of behavior. The notion of experience, for example; we can get along perfectly well without tracing the stimulus through the body. But some physiologists hope to find a copy of the external environment somewhere in the nervous system.

EVANS: Would this observation apply also to other recent developments in neurophysiology?

SKINNER: If it turns out that stimulation through implanted electrodes becomes a common variable altering behavior, then that will have to be taken into

account. The same is true of drugs. Operant conditioning techniques are widely used in assessing and
exploring behavioral drugs, and to this extent drugs
become, in a sense, new variables to be used in the
analysis of behavior. Of course, they are much more
interesting to the physiologist, and I think that's their
main significance.

EVANS: You seem to be making a fine distinction
between two types of language used to describe physiological research. One would be a form of what you
would describe as a fictional language which you apparently feel may actually *obstruct* clear understanding of behavior. The other language would reflect
behavior directly.

SKINNER: Yes. I am perfectly content to let the
physiologists go along by themselves. I should like to
help them if I can, but I strongly advise them to stop
trying to account for psychological fictions and get
down to the business of accounting for demonstrated
relationships between behavior and the independent
variables of which it is a function.

EVANS: Moving away from motivation and emotion, other areas in contemporary psychology that
continue to be of interest are sensation and perception. The more traditional research has always emphasized *disciplined* investigation of the sense organs,
such as vision. Today there seems to be increasing
concern with the nature of man's *naïve* experience or
the so-called phenomenological approach. How do
you account for this?

SKINNER: I think that the trend you mention is due
to the fact that what British Empiricists felt was going

to lead to an analysis of knowledge turned out to be a
matter for physiology, that is, how the end organs
work. But there remain all those curious activities
which are assigned to perception rather than sensa-
ation, where the end organs themselves don't seem to
account for the transformation between the physical
environment and something inside. The study of perception suffers from the notion that somehow or other
one is indeed relating experience to reality. People
look into a distorted room, for example, and see it one
way from one angle and another way from another,
and they feel they have seen it both as it appears to
be and as it really is. But that's nonsense. Both are
the way it seems to be, if you want to put it that way.
I don't at the moment particularly care about that
kind of experiment, because I don't feel that one
should answer the most difficult questions in a science
first. People study perception because they're in-
trigued by perceptual phenomena. The Gestalt psychologists have been studying intriguing visual
illusions for more than fifty years. New illusions are
added, and more people become fascinated by them,
but little real progress is made. There are subtleties
in perceptual phenomena which will have to wait to
be explained when our analytical machinery has become more powerful. I could guess how one would
deal objectively with size constancy, for example, but
I don't. I don't recommend anyone doing it now. I feel
that scientific progress comes about by a progression
from the more easily answered questions to the more
difficult.

EVANS: In your reference to the distorted room

experiment, you were saying that regardless of the *conditions* under which one views the situation, one still "sees" a distorted figure. This sounds a little like philosopher Immanuel Kant's (23) conception that there is no reality except man's perception of it, and I wondered if you intended to imply this?

SKINNER: No. I think in this matter I would do as Whitehead used to do. . . . I short-circuit Kant by going back to the British Empiricists. But I don't find myself very happy with either formulation.

EVANS: Of course, in your book *Verbal Behavior* (47), you have suggested that the study of verbal responses may be a fruitful approach to deal with the experiential, private, perceptual world of the individual.

SKINNER: I think an analysis which deals with verbal behavior without appealing to mental concepts such as meaning is a step in the right direction. A lot of behavioral phenomena, such as metaphor, bear striking resemblances to perceptual problems. I've not given up on perception, and in fact will talk about it with anyone who wants to talk about it. But I do feel that putting it so prominently in the forefront of psychology is a bit premature. I would say that in general, when one is studying a perceptual phenomenon, it is a question of exploring all the different kinds of stimuli which lead to a common response. Two objects which are "really" different are judged alike. I see no reason why any problem in perception cannot be converted into an exploration of the range of stimuli which give equivalent responses. But it is always a response that is being studied, not what you see. This is what is missed in physiological and psychological tracing of the stimulus through the body. Everyone seems to feel that somewhere in the brain there should be a copy of nature, and the perception people seem to feel that they are exploring the ways in which that copy differs from reality. But I insist that there is no copy there at all; that as soon as the organism begins to respond to the environment, it is responding and not duplicating, and that in seeing a triangle, for instance, there need be nothing in the organism which is triangular in any sense whatsoever, either physiologically, perceptually, or behaviorally. To study the perception of a triangle as what you see when you look at a triangle misses the point. The triangle you see is out there; it is not inside you; there is nothing to which you can relate a perceptual entity. The environment has triangles in it, and there are various ways in which we learn to react to triangles. When we were doing experiments with pigeons some time back, we taught pigeons to peck small triangles. We made a carbon copy of where they pecked, and found that when we gave them a big triangle to peck, they pecked in the corners. What the little triangles and the corners of the big triangle had in common directed the response. This kind of formulation, however, will not solve all our problems.

EVANS: You're speaking here, Dr. Skinner, about analyzing verbal responses as a means of getting at the perceptions of the individual. I am reminded of some earlier work of a different sort. You may recall that L. W. Max (30), among others, attempted to record *muscle* responses during various thought processes in individuals. How do you feel about this kind of response analysis?

SKINNER: One could approach behavior by analyzing the effects of contingencies on the response of a small muscle group. But the responses I deal with are the overt, molar responses of the organism to the environment, and I define response in terms of the effect on the environment. To my way of thinking, a study of what is going on in the muscles of the hand when it is responding, or the muscles of the speech apparatus when speaking, will not tell us much about the response itself.

EVANS: In other words, you feel that Max's approach to recording muscle response would really not be dealing with what you consider to be sufficiently molar response data.

SKINNER: No. That's muscle twitchism, and I don't see any point in it. Many people feel that in some way or other this type of analysis is more respectable and down to earth. It's true that the nervous system is earthy, whereas behavior seems to be evanescent, but the interesting things *are* evanescent, and one must deal with them as they pass. It's the nature of the subject matter, and must be dealt with as such.

EVANS: As you know, the electroencephalogram, or EEG, as it records electrical potentials of the brain has also been used in research in this field. Do you feel this may be a fruitful direction of research?

SKINNER: No. It may be possible to make some change in an EEG response by making something contingent on it, but what is going on in the EEG pattern during behavior is again part of the physiological story. It adds nothing to an account at the level of behavior.

EVANS: Moving away now from our discussion of perception, another major field of interest in contemporary psychology is learning. Central in any consideration of learning is the concept of conditioning as conceived by Pavlov (e.g., 34). How did Pavlov's work on the conditioned reflex affect your thinking as you began to develop your approach to learning?

SKINNER: Well, I certainly took off from the notion of the reflex and the conditioned reflex in the early years of my work as a psychologist. But I soon realized that something was wrong, and before the publication of *The Behavior of Organisms* (40), although I still used the word "reflex" more freely than I do now, the basic notion of an operant emerged. An operant is quite different from a reflex, and different from the Pavlovian conditioned reflex. My thinking has changed even more since then. I'm not at all sure how I would formulate the Pavlovian principle today. It was a curious accident, in one sense favorable and in another sense not favorable, that he hit upon the salivary reflex. There are not very many other responses which fit his paradigm, and many people have pointed out inconsistencies and difficulties in the Pavlovian analysis. This doesn't happen to interest me simply because I'm interested in behavior which does not *begin* as reflex or *become* reflex in Pavlov's sense.

EVANS: In discussing the intricacies in the conditioning process, many descriptive terms have been used by Pavlov and others. Of these terms, "instrumental" seems to best describe the kind of conditioning with which you are dealing. Yet you prefer the term "operant." Why not "instrumental"?

SKINNER: I don't think it's a very happy word because it implies the use of instruments, and there are units of behavior where the word is really not appropriate at all. I prefer to use the word "operant," in the sense of behavior which operates on the environment and produces reinforcing effects. You define an operant in terms of its effects, and study it by means of its effects on your apparatus. Operant behavior, as I see it, is simply a study of what used to be dealt with by the concept of purpose. The purpose of an act is the consequences it is going to have. Actually, in the case of operant conditioning, we study the consequences an act has had in the past. Changes in the probability of response are brought about when an act is followed by a particular kind of consequence. It can be positive or negative reinforcement as the case may be, but the datum that you watch and follow is the probability that a response of a given type will indeed occur. An operant, then, is a class of responses, and a response is a single instance of that class.

EVANS: In this analysis of operants, you obviously are concerned with temporal relationships when you speak of an act followed by a particular consequence. Such relationships, of course, were dealt with by Guthrie (17) in his concept of contiguity. Are you interested in contiguity?

SKINNER: Contiguity, in the sense that Guthrie used it, is not a concept that I'm particularly interested in. I use the word "contingencies" to describe the conditions which prevail at any given time and which relate a bit of behavior to its consequences. All the various kinds of complex equipment used in the laboratory are designed to arrange certain contingencies of reinforcement—so that when a response has a given topography it will indeed be followed by certain reinforcing events or will be followed by such an event on a certain schedule or will be followed by such an event only in the presence of a given stimulus, and so on. I view the study of operant behavior as essentially an exploration of the effects of all of the contingencies of reinforcement which are around in daily life or can be created in laboratories.

EVANS: Dr. Skinner, historically we have seen psychology deal with the stimulus-response, or S-R paradigm, as well as the stimulus-organism-response, or S-O-R paradigm. We find that these two paradigms are still developing concurrently. It appears to be difficult for the student of psychology to decide what is implied by being an S-R psychologist. Does this mean that everything that occurs within the organism or O—that mysterious "black box"—between the stimulus to which the individual is exposed and the response which it evokes is irrelevant for the student of behavior? To be scientific must we speak of an "empty organism"? How do you view this overall problem?

SKINNER: I think there are two issues here. Let me emphasize first that I do not consider myself an S-R psychologist. The stimulus is only one among a lot of different variables. As it stands, I'm not sure that response is a very useful concept. Behavior is very fluid; it isn't made up of lots of little responses packed together. I hope I will live to see a formulation which will take this fluidity into account. The stimulating environment is important among the variables of which behavior is a function, but it is by no means the only one. I don't like efforts to extend the concept of stimulus by considering as stimuli drive states, or conditions resulting from reinforcement. It is a mistake to suppose that there are internal stimuli and to try to formulate everything as S-R psychology. I don't think hunger, for example, should be considered a stimulus. There is stimulation associated with states of deprivation, but deprivation does not act by producing stimuli which then affect behavior. We have borrowed the stimulus-response pattern from reflex physiology, and it has served a useful purpose, but there is a more effective formulation. The topography of a response is only one property. If you take rate of responding as the datum, then details of any one response become less important. All you need is to be able to count successive instances in establishing a rate. Once you are observing the rate, you look around for anything which has an influence on it. Some of the influences will reasonably be described as stimuli, and some will not.

I think, however, that the problem goes deeper than that. If the O represents the organism and S-R represents input and output, then the question arises, How important is the O? I guess I'm even more opposed to postulating the influence of O than I am to the strict S-R formulation. As I see it, psychology is concerned with establishing relations between the behavior of an organism and the forces acting upon it. Now, the

organism must be there. . . . I don't really believe in
the "empty organism." That wasn't my phrase. But
the relationships that psychology discovers set the
problem which the physiologist must solve by filling
in the gaps. The variables we study are separated in
time and space, and something happens in between.
I hope that this particular something will be investi-
gated just as rapidly as possible. I have never said
anything against the study of physiology, and I feel
that I have done my best to facilitate it by clarifying
the problems that the physiologist has to deal with.
At the same time, I don't want to borrow support from
physiology when my formulation breaks down. If I
can't give a clean-cut statement of a relationship between behavior and antecedent variables, it is no help
to me to speculate about something inside the organism which will fill the gap. The gap is in my data. It is
something that I must eventually fill by improving
the analysis, not borrowing from somewhere else. As
far as I'm concerned, the organism is irrelevant either
as the site of physiological processes or as the locus
of mentalistic activities. I don't believe the organism
contributes anything to these overall relationships
beyond the fact that it is the behavior of an organism
we are studying. We begin with an organism as a
genetic product. It very quickly acquires a history,
and we, as students of behavior, must deal with it as
an organism with a history. If we find that we can
control some of these historical variables, then we do
so. If we can't, we try to deal with genetically stable
stock. We may raise an organism from birth under
controlled conditions in order to be sure of its genetic

inheritance. But we can't dispense with the fact that we are studying an organism. We need to study ethology and instinctive behavior. For some reason, the ethologists seem to be unhappy about what they are doing; they seem to feel their work is important only if it undercuts the analysis of learning. I don't know what they want us to do that we're not doing, but we certainly accept the fact that we are not beginning with an empty organism or a *tabula rasa*. Any representative member of a given species will have characteristics of the species. It will also have an individual history.

EVANS: Dr. Skinner, earlier, in referring to certain concepts you've used the word "irrelevant." Since in this context your use of the term could be subject to misinterpretation, would you mind clarifying for us what you mean by it?

SKINNER: When I say that a concept is irrelevant, I mean that it has no bearing on the kind of analysis I am trying to develop. It could conceivably bear on the mediation of the relationships I'm dealing with, but what I object to is the use of supposed mental or neurological activities to account for slips between the cup and the lip. I don't think inferred concepts adequately make up for things lacking in a behavioral analysis. We need a complete account at the external level. After all, the organism cannot initiate anything unless you assume it is capable of whimsical changes. As a determinist, I must assume that the organism is simply mediating the relationships between the forces acting upon it and its own output, and these are the kinds of relationships I'm anxious to formulate. As a matter of intellectual hygiene, I avoid slipping over into some other universe to patch up deficiencies in my analysis.

EVANS: Humanists often accuse behaviorists of having no concern for human values or human good because behaviorists view man as being merely a machine. Some of this criticism, no doubt, is based on works such as Clark Hull's *Principles of Behavior* (20) where he makes the statement, in the first chapter, that "for the purposes of analyzing behavior, we have to assume that man is a machine." Although Hull obviously didn't intend to state *literally* that he believed that man is a machine, this was interpreted to be his meaning even by many of his followers. For example, I remember in a learning course I once took from a proponent of Hull's, he would begin the course by asking, "How many of you believe man is a machine?" The ones who didn't raise their hands appeared to be considered "suspect" by that professor as not being real "scientists." How do you react to this criticism of behaviorism by the humanists?

SKINNER: If by "machine," you simply mean any system which behaves in an orderly way, then man and all the other animals are machines. But this has nothing to do with the interests of the humanists or of the interests of any man of compassion who deals with his fellowman. The behaviorists, like scientists in general, are attempting to reach certain goals. They use their own techniques to arrive at these goals, just as the humanist uses his own techniques to arrive at his goals. Though I call myself a behaviorist, I don't particularly like the term. However, we see that the humanist and the behaviorist have different conceptions of man and the nature of man. But if it is the goal which matters, rather than the conception, then I feel that the weight of evidence is all on our side. For example, in education we can specify materials and methods which bring about the changes in the student we want to bring about—and in a very effective way, much more effective than the person who thinks of the student simply as an individual whose wishes must be respected, who must make decisions, and so on. He may make decisions, but the forces which lead him to do so must be taken into account. People who have most respected the student as an individual have at some time or other confessed to a need to arrange conditions which lead him to want to do what he wants to do.

AVERSIVE VERSUS POSITIVE CONTROL OF BEHAVIOR

CHAPTER 2

Overview | This chapter deals with an elaboration of Professor Skinner's powerful system for controlling behavior based on the principles of operant conditioning.

One of the most fascinating notions that Skinner has put forth as a result of many years of important laboratory research is that aversive control is much less effective than positive control. Skinner contends that man in our society tends to be most generally controlled by the less effective negative or aversive reinforcers rather than by the more effective positive ones. Applying this, for example, to our school system, one might say that the process of education for the child may be more likely to proceed because of the threat of failure or punishment to which the child is exposed rather than in terms of the promise of success or reward.

In order to explore the implications of this problem, Professor Skinner and I discuss some of his systematic and precise means of shaping behavior through *positive* rather than *aversive* control. He discusses how positive reinforcement may operate in work situations, Freud's so-called defense mechanisms in reinforcement terms, and how a system of positive reinforcement can be applied to even such clinical problems as the treatment of various emotional disorders.

In Professor Skinner's novel, *Walden Two*, he has illustrated how a system of positive reinforcement might develop and maintain an ideal or utopian society. In this chapter Skinner also answers the criticism that this operant conditioning—positive control technique of shaping behavior destroys man's "spirit."

EVANS: Dr. Skinner, earlier you referred to yourself as a determinist. With the shifting away from the Freudian model of biological determinism to a more environmental-social-cultural determinism in contemporary psychology, there seems to be a parallel, increasing concern with the notion of self-responsibility. This might partially be a reaction to the effects of such environmental-social-cultural theories on society. The theories themselves become a rationalization or excuse for an individual's misbehavior. For example, juvenile delinquents, as satirized in the Broadway musical *West Side Story*, in the "Officer Krupke Song," were singing, "We're not responsible for our acts, social conditions are." I wonder where you stand in relation to this issue?

SKINNER: I'm not arguing for the organism's self-responsibility. But the distinction you make is really a shift from aversive control to positive reinforcement, and it's a very important issue. For example, if you try to control alcoholism by criticizing and

shaming the drunkard, he may conceivably learn to
avoid criticism by controlling himself. But if you say,
"Wait a minute, here. This is really a medical problem.
You have a disease," he may use this as an excuse to
avoid punitive action. The alternative to punishing
people who behave badly is to build a world in which
people are naturally good. Personal responsibility is
something which even people who believe in punitive
control don't understand, even though they may admire
those who behave well under adverse conditions. The
point is clearly made by my colleague, David McClelland, in a paper called "Psychoanalysis and Religious
Mysticism" (26). He points out that Freud is very
close to the Protestant Reformation as well as to the
Hasidic mystical tradition of the Jews. He makes the
point that both Freud and the Christian-Jewish mystic
are departing from orthodoxy in the sense of strict
disciplinary control and are turning toward inner
sources of control. The early Christians and Jews, in
the Kumran community and the monasteries, were
submitting themselves to external authority in order to
control themselves. In the Dead Sea Scrolls, obedience
was the thing; as it was for the Benedictines and other
monastic orders. You put yourself under a punishing
authority and are then responsible for your actions in
the sense that if you do not behave properly you will
be justly punished. That's all the word "responsible"
means; it has no meaning in a society which does not
control through aversive techniques. In the Hasidic
movement and with Freud, it is not that inner sources
of control have been substituted for the external,
authoritative, orthodox sources, but that there has

been a shift from negative reinforcement to positive reinforcement. People do what they want to do rather than what they have to do. The same goals are achieved—they do the same things. It's not internal control but a different kind of external control.

The notion of personal responsibility just isn't relevant. The control is still there. When you turn the delinquent over to himself, as some psychologists and psychiatrists feel you can do, you will be successful only if society has in some way implanted the kinds of control which are essential. This is a point on which I argue with Carl Rogers, who claims that somehow or other you are going to find within the client himself the controlling forces that will solve his problem. His methods work with clients who have emerged from a tradition, such as the Judeo-Christian, which gives them reasons for behaving well, but if a client suddenly announces, "Ah, yes! I see it now. I should murder my boss!" you don't just let him walk out of the office. You don't tell him that he has really found the solution to his problem. Every solution comes from some source of control. If his problem was generated by overly strict aversive control, your aim is to release him from that, but you can't therefore turn him over to nothing. You don't turn him over to absolute freedom.

EVANS: Your emphasis on positive reinforcement, then, might be said to be reflecting an already existing historical-cultural trend away from aversive control toward positive control.

SKINNER: Yes. I'm really a little embarrassed to say this, because I don't believe in arguing from history.

However, I do think it is interesting to watch what is going on, even though I don't like to make predictions on historical evidences. Civilization has moved from an aversive control toward a positive approach. There are only a few places in the world today where slavery is still practiced, where labor is coerced by the whip. We have substituted the payment of wages for physical punishment, and are even concerned with finding other reinforcers. We should like to have a man work productively for the sheer love of it, and we reflect back on the old craft system as an example. You hear claims occasionally that we've got to start whipping our school boys and girls again, but this simply reminds us that until very recently, education was openly aversive. Egyptians, Greeks, and Romans all whipped their boys, and, in fact, the Latin expression for study means to hold out the hand to be whipped. In England, the cane is still used, but there is a movement away from punishment, and an effort to find positive reasons for studying. The same is true in religion. There is less and less emphasis on hell-fire and the threat of damnation; people are to be good for positive reasons, for the love of God or their fellowmen. There is a parallel trend in politics and in government. In a famous case in the thirties the Agricultural Act provided that farmers be paid for not planting acreage, instead of making it illegal to plant. This was an effort to avoid a coercive threat. It was an important trend, and supported because people generally don't like to be punished. And on a more intimate level, we prefer to have people get along well with each other because their outgoing, positive behavior is richly reinforcing rather than because they are afraid of being criticized or punished for misbehaving. I'm not a historical determinist to the point at which I would predict that this trend is going to continue, but I hope it does. A punitive society is not supported by the people under it, whereas a society which is full of good things is likely to be strong.

EVANS: I know, Dr. Skinner, that your experimental work led you to make distinctions among the conceptions of *punishment, negative reinforcement,* and *aversive control.* Could you discuss these distinctions?

SKINNER: You can distinguish between punishment, which is making an aversive event contingent upon a response, and negative reinforcement, in which the elimination or removal of an aversive stimulus, conditioned or unconditioned, is reinforcing. Aversive control is a way of generating behavior. When you say you punish a child to make him work, you are misusing the word "punish." You are arranging conditions which he can escape from by working. When you punish a child to keep him from misbehaving, however, you are trying to suppress behavior. In my earlier experiments punishment did not suppress behavior as it had been supposed to do. Punishment may only be reducing a current tendency to respond. As soon as punishment is withdrawn, the behavior bounces back. This isn't always the case, because extremely severe punishment may knock behavior out for good, at least so far as we are able to determine. But what is surprising is that if you make common punishing events contingent on behavior, the be-

havior will recover after the punishment ceases, and
the organism will continue to behave, even though it
has been rather severely punished. I object to aversive control in general because of its by-products. All
sorts of emotions are generated which have negative
side effects. If you make a student study to escape
punishment, then he will soon escape in other ways;
he'll play hookey, be a truant, or become a dropout.
Or he may counterattack. Vandalism against school
property is easily explained just by looking at the
techniques schools use to control their students. Another common reaction of students is a kind of in-
activity—an apathy or stubborn do-nothingness. These
are the inevitable by-products of aversive stimuli.
Positive reinforcement does not generate comparable
by-products, and that's why it's better. If we knew as
much about negative reinforcement as we do about
positive, I suspect we would find that it can be rather
effective in shaping behavior, but at the moment it
isn't very effective, and the negative by-products are
still in evidence, so I am opposed to it.

EVANS: But aversive control still seems to be the
order of the day in our entire culture. We see it in
laws, regulations, rules, salary schedules, and even in
the grading system we use in our schools. Supposing
we would like to shift to a more positively controlled
system. Is there any way that we could gradually
shift from our present system to a system based more
on positive reinforcement?

SKINNER: There are always transitional problems
when you shift from one framework to another, and
usually they are quite troublesome. To use your ear-

lier example, the delinquent simply pleads that he is a crazy, mixed-up kid and should be forgiven, that it isn't his fault. If you are going to control delinquency simply by punishment, then you've got to stick to that and call the delinquent guilty. He has been irresponsible, he is at fault, and he must be punished. To attempt to deal with the situation any other way will mean a transitional period in which your control is likely to be bad. It is at this point that the delinquent will choose your new formulation as an easy way to escape punishment. You can't blame him for taking advantage of the changing situation. That's predictable human behavior.

EVANS: What about *extinction* in dealing with undesirable behavior?

SKINNER: Well, extinction is another way of getting rid of undesirable behavior. But in order for it to be effective, you must be sure that no reinforcing consequences are contingent on the behavior you want to get rid of. Generally, it isn't very effective. It takes a long time, and you have to put up with the behavior while you are getting rid of it. I would prefer to use a method which reinforces incompatible behavior. Very interesting work has been done recently in teaching discrimination without errors; it involves both avoiding the reinforcement of wrong responses and using stimuli for right responses as reinforcers. The research has promise in the direction you have indicated here. The area has scarcely been developed, because we've only begun to look for alternatives to punishment. Punishment is the easy way—if you're strong enough. If the teacher is bigger than his stu-

dent, he can resort to punishment and get away with
it.

EVANS: Any discussion of systems of control in
society, of course, raises questions of what systems of
control actually operate in communist societies. For
example, how about the Soviet Union?

SKINNER: I'm not too impressed by what I've seen
in the Soviet Union; and theoretically, I think they are
wrong. I don't think they even subscribe to their own
theory. Marx's principle, "to each according to his
need," is, of course, scriptural; it is not St. Karl; it's St.
Augustine. But the principle misses the boat because
the important thing is what a man does at the moment
he receives what he needs. That's where reinforcement
comes in. Anyone can sympathize with a person who
is hungry and, out of simple compassion, feed him.
That's a good thing, I'm all for it. I'm not for starving
people in order to make them productive. In Victorian
England, it was supposed that you would have to
have a population of nearly starved workers in order
to maintain production in the factories of the time.
And it may have been necessary then, because work
was very aversive. But I think the Russian principle
also has been abandoned. Khrushchev reportedly told
the then Senator Humphrey that the "crazy Chinese"
still believed you should give to each according to his
need. Yet Khrushchev promised the Russian people
that by 1980 food, housing, clothing would be free. If
he actually meant free, that these things are to be
given away and not made contingent on productive
labor, then there will be no reason for people to work.
I once argued this with a Russian economist whom I

met at a reception in England. I said, "If this happens, why will a man work?" He took a very smug stance, and said, "Ah, they will work for the common good." But as Karl Marx himself knew, there is a great gap between working at a given moment and participation in the common good at a later date. The Russians need some sort of incentive system. The Russian worker in general is not as productive as the American worker, and it can't be explained just on the basis of a dearth of capital equipment in Russia.

EVANS: All of the properties of this incentive system would not necessarily be positively reinforcing, would they? There would likely also be some aversive elements in the system, as I understand your meaning here, wouldn't there?

SKINNER: Oh, yes. Many people, and textbooks as well, cite the weekly wage as an example of a scheduled positive reinforcement, but actually that's quite wrong. If you reinforce a man only at five o'clock on Friday afternoon, he will work only, say, from five minutes before five to five o'clock. The reason he works on Mondays is that if he doesn't he'll be fired; he will be unable to collect his money on Friday afternoon. A schedule of payment established on an hourly, daily, or weekly basis must involve some kind of supervision in order to be effective. There must be a boss around who has the power to fire a worker and thereby cut him off from the standard of living established by that periodic pay. It is basically an aversive system. People don't actually feel strengthened by a weekly wage as a reinforcer; they work because if they don't they will be cut off from a supply of reinforcers. It's an unhealthy system. There's another schedule I've studied in some detail, the fixed-ratio schedule of reinforcement. It's seen in operation in the piece-rate system, where the worker is paid in terms of the amount of work he does. This does not require supervision, and on this type of schedule, an organism will indeed start work long before reinforcement because he must start if he is to reach the point of being reinforced. Actually, that schedule is so powerful that most labor unions oppose it; it can burn a man up—exhaust him. The home industry in nineteenth-century England operated on that basis. The house-wife put the kiddies to bed, then got out a machine and knitted up a few socks, for which she got paid a penny a dozen, or something like that. It was a horrible system, but it commanded productive work. There's no doubt about that.

Incentive systems are a mixture of the two schedules.[1] There is enough of the periodic pay to provide a satisfactory base so that the ratio-type schedule doesn't completely take over. A salesman who is partly on a salary and partly on commission is an example of the way these systems can be combined. The salary he earns takes the edge off the commission basis, so he

[1]To review for the reader to what Skinner is referring: There are two broad schedules of reinforcement that have been used as a means of increasing the probability that certain behavior will occur. One is called a *ratio* schedule, the other is called an *interval* schedule. When reinforcements are introduced on a *ratio* schedule, a certain number of responses must occur before the organism is reinforced (similar to piece-work for a worker). An *interval* schedule is introduced according to the clock or calendar—say every so many minutes in an experiment, but for a worker it could be his weekly paycheck.

can live a sensible life without forcing himself. He doesn't have to have a supervisor traveling along with him, because the commission is on a ratio schedule, and that will keep him going. A proper mixture of salary and commission yields productive work which is also free of supervision, yet without the excessive effects of a ratio schedule in a piecework system. These are just examples of the application to economics of behavioral processes studied in the laboratory. What we do in the laboratory, of course, is extremely technical, and often complex, but it points to systems that would generate almost any level of activity on the part of a worker or student—anyone, for that matter, who is being reinforced by what he is doing.

EVANS: As you reflect further on the differences in the systems operating in the United States and the Soviet Union, do you see problems emerging for the Soviets when the incentives for productive work are withdrawn and no positive reinforcements are introduced that go beyond a formalized theoretical base?

SKINNER: I think the problem is already there. The Russians are already charging their educators with the responsibility of imparting the attitudes needed to keep people working productively. And that isn't going to work. To keep people working imaginatively, actively, and in a sustained fashion for something as abstract as a verbalized reinforcer called the "common good," or the feeling that one is engaging in socially useful behavior, is a terrific engineering job. The Soviets do not presently have such an engineered system, and while ours is not perfect, we're at least better off. Our wage systems are defective in that they breed various unwanted reactions on the part of workers. Few people enjoy working on a modern production line, but if the hours can be cut down far enough and the wages raised high enough, they can at least enjoy the rest of their lives. Much more could be done to make what they do on the job more interesting. Piping music into a factory is by no means enough. Good working conditions that include social effects which give the individual some sense of achievement can be made to pay off in a rather artificial, but healthier way. These are all possibilities, and should be exploited. A crude example is the so-called variable ratio schedule, which is at the heart of all gambling devices. We might try giving workers lottery tickets based on production, in addition to their ordinary wages, with a drawing at the end of the week. People enjoy wasting money and time and energy on gambling if it pays off at least occasionally, so why not incorporate similar schedules into industrial systems?

EVANS: A sort of "gambling model" of reinforcement of the worker in industry.

SKINNER: There is nothing wrong with the schedule. All scientific work pays off on a variable ratio schedule. So do hunting, fishing, exploring, prospecting, and so on. You never can tell when you are going to be reinforced, but reinforcements do keep turning up. The dedicated scientist is exactly like a pathological gambler. He's been hooked by a system, but in a way which is profitable for everyone. The scientist is fascinated by what he does, just as the gambler is, but nobody is taking his shirt. He's getting something out of it, and so is society.

EVANS: Gambling seems to have a unique sort of fascination for most people. It's interesting to observe in Las Vegas how really powerful the intermittent-variable reinforcement schedule apparently operating in "games of chance" is for most people.

SKINNER: Yes. I've seen people playing three or four machines at one time, going right down the line keeping them all whirring. Industry would give any-thing to command sustained effort like that. Actually, those machines could be ch nged so that they would clean out the pockets of the patrons even faster. I could design a better gambling machine—better from the point of view of the establishment—but I won't.

EVANS: Moving to another area, Freud identified a group of defense mechanisms to attempt to describe certain kinds of behavior employed by an individual to avoid, at least psychologically, the consequences of aversive, ego-threatening situations. You have exam-ined the Freudian defense mechanisms, have you not? Can they also be regarded as examples of aversive control?

SKINNER: Yes, I have analyzed the Freudian mech-anisms (44), and in a sense, I attribute them all to aversive control. They represent ways of avoiding un-desirable consequences of one sort or another, and when analyzed in that light, they suggest means of correction. If, instead of building up the behavior you want in people, you punish the behavior you don't want, the individual must discover ways which do indeed avoid the punishing consequences. But these may not be effective ways; they may be called neu-rotic. Society might better build effective behavior. When you simply punish the slothful student for his sloth, the ignorant student for his ignorance, and the willful student for his willfulness, you leave it to the student to figure out ways of avoiding punishment. What he does is largely a matter of accident. On the other hand, you can reinforce his behavior so that he becomes energetic and far from slothful; you can program instruction to lead him out of his ignorance; you can induce him to behave according to the dictates of society instead of his own selfish interests. You have solved the problems of sloth, ignorance, and willfulness by constructing desirable behaviors. Positive shaping of behavior is much the more successful way.

EVANS: Isn't this type of positive shaping of response and environmental manipulation being systematically applied in psychotherapy? Of course, some have challenged this method by saying that it ignores the "private world" of the patient and reduces his interaction with the therapist and his environment to such a mechanical, superficial level that the deep, underlying "psychodynamics" of his problem are ignored. How do you feel about this sort of criticism?

SKINNER: I don't think you really lose out on anything. A psychotic patient is psychotic because of his behavior. You don't institutionalize a person because of his feelings. You may say that behavior is a result of his feelings, but the feelings must be the result of something, too. When you look farther, you find environmental factors. I do not rule out the possibility of genuine internal illness, but illness in that sense is not the rich experience which I am accused of leaving out. I see nothing demeaning, nothing undignified or ignoble, about building a world in which a psychotic person can lead a decent life. True, it may be a simplified world. Many psychotics are certainly sick or damaged organisms, and they can never successfully return to an ordinary environment. But under the control of simplified environments, their lives can then be happier and possibly more productive.

EVANS: What you're suggesting would apply not only to psychotherapy but also to the patient within an institutional situation. There has been some work done (3) attempting to bring the mentally ill within the hospital setting under various reinforcement schedules which will bring them to a point where they can function more effectively and assume greater self-responsibility. Do you feel such efforts are going to prove increasingly fruitful?

SKINNER: I'm sure they're on the right track.

EVANS: How could these efforts be made most effective?

SKINNER: There are two possibilities: One is to eliminate the poor contingencies which now prevail in those institutions—where, for example, it is the troublemaker who is reinforced by getting the attention of the hospital attendants. The alternative is to be much more explicit about it and build a world which is admittedly contrived. It will not be a natural environment; but these are not natural cases. You can contrive a situation in which such people will live reasonably effective lives from day to day with a minimum of care. When you have to keep people clean and orderly against their own contributing negligence, it is expensive, and everyone suffers. There's not a great deal of money available for the care of psychotics. If you reorganize their environment so that their behavior is more effective without the constant intervention of attendants, you can give them a better life with the facilities available. To my way of thinking, this is *increasing* their dignity and nobility. It's true that they're being controlled in a rather artificial way, but if the life they then lead is reasonably adequate, I regard that as a success.

EVANS: Similar methods are being applied to the mentally retarded. Do you feel the same way about this area of application?

SKINNER: Yes. Several of my colleagues and I have experimented with institutionalized retardates whose IQ's ranged around 50 (whatever that may mean). They respond well to a simplified environment, and I am sure that institutions which care for them could be reorganized along the same lines. At the present time, retardates tend to be controlled through aversive techniques, even though the attendants may be full of goodwill. No one really benefits from that. I believe that the institutionalized retardate, just below the level needed to operate in the world at large, can be placed in an environment in which he will not only live reasonably happily all day long, but will also be productive. These people are capable of performing certain kinds of work, and actually of making a living. They can enjoy happier circumstances which they actually pay for by their efforts.

EVANS: Aren't you suggesting that some of the existing conceptions of mental retardation underestimate the potential for training the retardate actually possesses?

SKINNER: No doubt about that at all. This is true of all organisms. I know one psychologist who tried to work with pigeons who couldn't teach them anything. In the last twenty years, pigeons have done things no pigeon had ever done before. It isn't that the pigeons have been improved; the contingencies under which they live have been improved. A retardate doesn't measure up to the normal environment and can't get along within it, but he is capable of perfectly acceptable behavior in an environment which has been designed for him.

EVANS: There is another broad area which it would be interesting to hear your reaction to, Dr. Skinner, and that is your concept of the role of psychology in the interpretation of literature and in creative writing. So far this field seems to have been dominated by Freudian theory. I wonder if you feel that some training in experimental analysis of behavior would be of help to the creative writer?

SKINNER: I used to be interested in Freudian interpretations of the themes of literature, as well as the themes of history and biography. I find myself much less inclined to take analyses seriously any more, because they fall into stereotyped patterns and I get awfully tired of them. But you have raised two questions. Can a writer make use of our knowledge of verbal behavior to improve his product or to maximize his productivity? I am sure that the answer is "yes." The other question is whether it is possible to design writing in such a way that the reader will almost certainly read it, and will be influenced by what he reads. I think the answer to that question is also "yes." I take special steps to maximize my verbal output. This does not mean maximizing quantity; it means arranging conditions under which I am most likely to write effectively. I catch my verbal behavior on the wing, as it were, and get it down as soon as it occurs. Then I rework it later when time permits. But these are technical details which are not appropriate here. On the side of the reader—reinforcing passages can be scheduled to keep him reading.

EVANS: This is true also for the electronic communications media, is it not? In fact, it would seem that a good deal of advertising on television and radio is the outgrowth of a hopefully effectively scheduled array of reinforcers.

SKINNER: I only hope what has been done so far is not the best that can be done, because on the whole it's pretty dreary stuff. I could probably write better copy, but I am no more inclined to help advertisers than gamblers.

EVANS: Fears concerning this whole notion of the possibility of controlling the environment because it could pervade an entire culture were brought out in the controversy which followed the publication of your highly successful novel, *Walden Two*. Such a "planned utopia" seemed to be particularly distressing to the humanist. As you conceived the culture you wrote about in *Walden Two*, did you seriously believe such a society would actually come into being?

SKINNER: I wrote the book quite seriously. It is not a dystopia. I thought such a community was possible at the time I wrote the book, and I think so now. It should be possible for a group of well-meaning people to get together and organize their lives, cutting down some of the things they normally consume to eliminate some of the aversive labors otherwise required; to organize their social environment so that they make more contacts of a satisfactory nature; to organize a school system which educates their children effectively for the life they are going to lead; to organize an economic system so that work can at least be done under pleasant circumstances; and so on. But when I described such a society, reaction was quite violent. *Life* magazine called *Walden Two* a triumph of mortmain, or the dead hand, such as had not been envisaged since the days of Sparta. Joseph Wood Krutch (25) not only devoted half a book to attacking it, he has returned to the attack on many occasions. I've often asked myself what's eating these people? Apparently the main difficulty is that my good life was planned by someone. If Joseph Wood Krutch were one day to climb up on a mesa in his beloved New Mexico, and come across a small civilization living the life described in *Walden Two*, he would come down out of the hills saying, "What fools we are! Here is the perfect life." But if someone told him that an old Indian named Frazier* had designed that life, it would spoil it all for him. The fact that a way of life is not the product of a series of accidents in cultural evolution but has been designed suggests that someone is in the position of designer and, therefore, in the position of a threatening despot. But there are kinds of guarantees against despotism within any system; if there aren't, then we are without hope in any way of life.

EVANS: Allow me to play devil's advocate for a

---

* The character in *Walden Two* who guides the development of the utopian community.

moment. Isn't it possible that such fears of despotism connected with a planned society have their referents in recent history? Attempts to plan a society could be found, of course, in Nazi Germany, the Soviet Union, and China. According to its planners, each system was designed to hopefully allow a climate of creative productivity so that each individual would operate at his most comfortable and productive level. These goals would appear to be in accord with the philosophical concept of the "good life." Yet the results of such planning in these countries, while it may be thought to be oriented toward the "good life," actually seemed to have evolved into a despotic system. How do we guarantee that the type of planning you propose will not ulimately also produce a despotic system?

SKINNER: This is the old question of value judgments. What values are we to use in judging one society good and another bad? You first question the techniques. If you govern by coercion, as the Nazis did, waking people up in the middle of the night and dragging them off to jail, you can control for a period of time, but you are controlling frightened people. Moreover, you do not encourage support from the outside. Eventually the method fails. I believe that the Russians are trying to avoid that kind of control; they've had a long history of it, and seem now to be trying to use positive reinforcement, though they are not organizing their contingencies properly.

I don't know what's going on in China today, since we're not allowed to know much. But I suspect that the Chinese are a lot closer to Karl Marx than the Russians. The Chinese probably have to fall back on coercive control from time to time, and I'm sure that they have not discovered the contingencies which make positive reinforcement successful. The primary product is successful control, but the by-product may be that those controlled are working at less than their maximum capacity. If you control through superstition and ignorance, as has been the case in India, the control may be profound (a maharaja and his descendants may prevail for centuries) but it is the control of ignorant people, and that doesn't make for a strong state. In the long run you have to consider the survival of the group, and the despot who controls through techniques which weaken the group eventually weakens himself. I don't know whether a real leader will ever realize, as Frazier did, that his power depends entirely on the strength of the people. Frazier is not currently ruling at all. He has no control. People don't know who he is. And when he asks the young architects to come around to talk with his friends, they go off swimming. True, he did put the whole thing in motion, but he didn't do that for his own aggrandizement; if he had done it for that reason, he would have failed. He has successfully suppressed himself as a leader; that was a deliberate point in the book, and I feel it is very important.

EVANS: Cultural anthropological studies have shown that most societies do operate out of systems of aversive control. Might there not be some, however, such as the Pueblo Indians, who operate out of a less aversive system than ours, which might supply valuable data on the kind of society to which you refer in *Walden Two*?

SKINNER: I don't believe nature ever performs an

experiment the right way. You might find a group in
New Mexico or the South Seas where there seems to
be very little competition, but you cannot argue that
their happiness stems from that, because there will be
a great many other things peculiar to the culture. You
can't prove anything with examples. I should be very
much surprised if a culture based on positive reinforcement were to come about by accident, because
too many things favor aversive control. Aversive techniques are immediate, and they always work provided one person is stronger than another. The bully
dominates the coward. The powerful man rules,
especially when he can organize henchmen to help
him dominate. It is easy to account for such control,
because the effects are immediate. The results of positive reinforcement are often deferred, and so control
by this means is not as effective. It's the same in education; the teacher wants the student to be quiet and
study, so she threatens and gets results. But once the
student is released from that kind of pressure, he'll
never study again. If he can be induced to study for
other reasons, using reinforcing consequences which
will persist in his life, the results will be more lasting.
But that requires a much better understanding of
human behavior.

EVANS: On the other hand, leadership in pre-
literate societies seems to be based on physical dominance.

SKINNER: Yes, and then followed by trickery. The
first hero is the power man, the Beowulf. Then comes
the tricky hero, the Brer Rabbit, who puts it over on
Brer Wolf and Brer Bear by violating the code of the

group. Most cultures seem to have a cheating hero at some stage. Eventually someone gains control for the good of the controllee, and that is the genesis of a powerful group. It isn't the ruler who is powerful; it is the unit as a whole. Powerful but careless rulers lack the support of a powerful group.

EVANS: Leadership by dominance is a phenomenon which shows up even in the subhuman orders, as studies demonstrating the pecking order in chickens have shown. So even this can be viewed as essentially a system of aversive control.

SKINNER: It is a natural thing.

EVANS: Are you saying, then, that this aversive control, or control by dominance, is a more primitive, generic method, and that societies have evolved out of this root into what we have today?

SKINNER: I don't know whether the human organism is innately endowed so that he flies into a rage when someone harms him, but he certainly shows a strong tendency to do that. Our way of life encourages it because you often get what you want when you fly into a rage. People who annoy you then leave you alone. I suspect that it is an acquired response, however, because we are much more likely to get mad at people than at things. If you walk down a street and your way is blocked by several hippies who refuse to move, you may react with resentment and anger and say something to them if you dare. You may not attack them then and there, but you may suggest passing a law to keep people from blocking the sidewalk. But if you go down a street and find that a tree has fallen across it, you walk around the tree and feel no tendency to aggressively attack. This suggests that we have acquired our angers because they have paid off. Getting angry at a tree is not often reinforced. If we can build a world in which rage doesn't pay off, it will be a world in which people don't fly into a rage at the slightest annoyance.

EVANS: Is it possible that at least one effect of some of our theological teachings tends to reinforce the notion of aversive control?

SKINNER: Religions seem to move toward a positive kind of control through love and goodwill, but they certainly begin with jealous and punitive gods. I think the change in religion has been as great as in government and economics.

EVANS: The notion of aversive control seems to be so much taken for granted that there is seldom any question about it.

SKINNER: Practically all forms of governments are based on it. When you try something else, peculiar things happen. An interesting experiment was once done in New Haven. Instead of giving people tickets when they went through stop signs, someone stood around taking the numbers of those who stopped. As I remember it, they sent postcards saying, "You were observed to come to a dead stop at such and such an intersection on such and such a date. Congratulations." Something like that might increase the number of dead stops, but naturally it will not control the real lawbreaker. The procedure is so far out, though, that people laugh when they hear about it. It just doesn't seem appropriate for a government to operate through positive reinforcement.

EVANS: As you speak of shaping human resources, this brings to mind disturbing possibilities which result from so-called brainwashing American soldiers by the Chinese, such as described by Schein (39) in the Korean war. You developed a methodology to shape behavior which appears to be incredibly effective. How can we deal with the problem of how it's going to be used? It is certainly available to anyone who chooses to use it, so how can it be controlled?

SKINNER: There is a real danger here. From what I've heard of the Chinese prison-camp methods, they don't seem to have been very original. I doubt that there was anything done in China which was not known to Torquemada in the Spanish Inquisition. The same techniques were used for the same purposes. But it is conceivable that ways of influencing human behavior can be worked out which will not breed revolt, and that is the crucial danger. When people are being pushed around, controlled by methods which are obvious to them, they know who and what is controlling them, and when things become too aversive, they turn against the controller.

EVANS: You've argued that such aversive controls never had any sustained value anyway.

SKINNER: When you know what is being done to you, you know where to turn in order to escape. But some kinds of drugs and some kinds of positive reinforcement can be used without identifying the controller. Even though you are inclined to revolt, you don't know whom to revolt against. You do revolt against positive reinforcement, of course, if it gets you into trouble. A hobby may become so engaging that you lose interest in other things and risk destroying your career. You may then revolt against the hobby. But that is possible because you can identify what is controlling you. But it is conceivable that techniques of control will be developed which cannot be discovered. The word "brainwashing" is dangerous. I don't believe, however, that there's any great danger at the present time.

EVANS: The principles which you outlined so carefully in your *Science and Human Behavior* (43) could become quite effective if, say, a hostile government were to gain control and proceed to shape the development of children, putting such techniques totally into use. Could this not lead to a rather dangerous situation for the world?

SKINNER: There's no doubt about it, but what are you going to do? To impose a moratorium on science would be worst of all. It does not solve the problem to say we must not increase our knowledge or publish what we already know because it might fall into the hands of despots. The best defense I can see is to make all behavioral processes as familiar as possible. Let everyone know what is possible, what can be used against them.

EVANS: It seems that the same danger inherent in the technology of nuclear weapons may be potentially inherent in the science of behavior.

SKINNER: I think a science of behavior is just as dangerous as the atom bomb. It has the potential of being horribly misused. We must devote ourselves to a better governmental design which will have some control over all destructive instruments.

EVANS: An interesting parallel to this discussion is shown in Goebbels' diary (16) as he outlined the entire formula of communications control in Nazi Germany. Many of the techniques he describes reflect the principles of reinforcement that you have written about.

SKINNER: Oh, yes. The Nazis made good use of the social sciences even though they had driven out most of the good people. It was "good" from their point of view, of course; dangerous from ours.

THE FORMAL EDUCATIONAL SYSTEM

CHAPTER 3

Overview | In this chapter Dr. Skinner and I discuss his innovative contribution to our educational system, the teaching machine. Also discussed is how it emerged from Skinner's unique conceptions of operant conditioning, based on positive reinforcement. His method involves scheduling rewards for children for learning a specially programmed progressive sequence of material at their own rate.

In this section, Professor Skinner also reacts to many of the crucial questions which face our educational system today. This includes his reaction to the so-called content-versus-method problem, that is, is it more important to be concerned with *what* the teacher teaches or *how* he teaches.

Dr. Skinner and I also discuss how he would go about changing the educational system along the lines which he proposes, that is, a system based on positive rather than aversive control. Skinner also discusses such problems as possible overconformity in the school system.

EVANS: Dr. Skinner, to turn now to the field of education, I know this to be an area which is of profound interest to you. You were the significant developer of programmed learning. In decribing this method of teaching, do you not use the term "teaching machines"?

SKINNER: Yes, I'm afraid I'm responsible for it. People advised me not to use the term, but a sewing machine sews, a washing machine washes, and a teaching machine teaches. The original teaching machines were the equipment in operant laboratories which arranged contingencies of reinforcement. That's all teaching is, arranging contingencies which bring above changes in behavior. Machines bring them about more rapidly than the natural contingencies in daily life. The teacher expedites learning by arranging effective contingencies, at least in theory. The contingencies arranged without instrumental aid are often quite defective. You can teach much more effectively with devices of one kind or another. In the future they will be commonplace in all instructional situations.

EVANS: Let's take a familiar everyday example of this, Dr. Skinner, and see how it works. Supposing a teacher in an elementary school does a careful job of teaching arithmetic in a progressive sequence and is considered a competent teacher. Would you say that even intuitively she could be arranging reinforcement schedules in a reasonably adequate manner?

SKINNER: She might be, but I wouldn't say the schedules could be called reasonably adequate. Of course, if she is teaching at all, she is arranging schedules of reinforcement. But programming isn't just a question of breaking a subject into a progressive series of small steps.

EVANS: That's an important point, as I see it, because so many people feel that merely programming material in a progressive sequence achieves the reinforcement that you describe. What other elements are there that affect the efficiency of learning?

SKINNER: In the first place, there is the progressive shaping of a complex response. I sometimes give a classroom demonstration with a hungry pigeon and a food dispenser. I ask the class what they want to see the pigeon do—within reason, of course—and in a matter of minutes, the pigeon is pacing a figure eight, or bowing to the audience, or what have you. It is a simple matter of operating the food dispenser at the right time. You can't wait for the pigeon to pace a figure eight before you reinforce it; you'd wait forever. You choose any response which will contribute to that figure eight. You select from available responses any which will lead to the response you are to produce. That is one kind of programming. Another kind of programming brings the response under the control of a particular stimulus. The pigeon paces a figure eight only when the light is on, say, and not when it is off. Stimulus control can be programmed and a lot of time saved in the process. Another kind of programming brings behavior under the control of intermittent reinforcement. If you devise an apparatus which reinforces every hundredth response, and put an organism in it, the organism will starve because it will not make the required one hundred responses. But if you reinforce every response, then every second response, then every fifth, then every tenth, twenty-fifth, fiftieth, and hundredth, you can get a pigeon to go on indefinitely, responding one hundred times for each small measure of food. Actually, you can build up to ten thousand responses for each small measure of food. But it takes programming. You can't reach the final stage without going through intervening stages. In most studies of learning, organisms are plopped down into terminal contingencies of reinforcement and allowed to struggle through. They may reach the terminal behavior or they may not. It is called trial and error, but that term doesn't really describe a behavioral process at all.

EVANS: You mentioned before that a teacher would have to be using some kind of reinforcement schedules or she really wouldn't be teaching at all. What specific reinforcers might be used in our hypothetical example of teaching arithmetic?

SKINNER: The teacher doesn't have too many reinforcers at her disposal. That's one of the tragedies of education. There are a number of contrived reinforcers, such as prizes or tokens, pats on the back, approval, attention, and that sort of thing. But the important thing is that the child sees that he is progressing toward some ultimately desirable state, even if only the state of getting through school. Any little indication of progress, such as being right so that you can move on to the next step, is enough. I don't define a reinforcer in any biological sense. Some reinforcers have an obvious relevance to biological conditions; some don't. The human organism is reinforced simply by being effective. It is reinforcing to the student to be right, but in a contemporary classroom he is seldom right and therefore receives little reinforcement. Possibly, for this type of student, something a little more important than being right must be brought into play, but there are other things which can be used.

EVANS: Your mention of "being right" as a reinforcer is very interesting. You are not suggesting that this is something "internal" or "self-satisfying" in the individual, are you? If so, this would suggest a circularity in the system.

SKINNER: No. All reinforcers are defined by their effects. It's not circular any more than saying that some metals can be magnetized and others cannot. We classify events according to their demonstrable effects on a given organism. Some of these events will have a plausible bearing on physiology, and some will not.

EVANS: So far we have talked about the programming of fairly simple or elementary subject matter. I wonder to what degree effective programming could be carried out in the case of more complex, abstract subject matter. Take, for example, a course in epistemology. In this field, at least at the graduate level, there often may not be any "right" answers, and it would appear to be a little difficult to program a rigorous sequence.

SKINNER: Anything that can be verbalized can be programmed. (Important things can also be taught, of course, which are not verbal at all.) If you can verbalize epistemology, you can teach it. It might be embarrassing to put down the so-called right answers. I'm not sure there are any.

EVANS: Those who have been critical of the programming approach would argue that you are losing something over and above that which can be reduced to a precisely organized series of responses, which may be supplied even by a poor teacher.

SKINNER: A student does get something out of a bad teacher. He discovers how to learn in spite of a bad teacher. Obviously he doesn't learn this with a good teacher. It's quite true that in learning programmed material a student will not be learning some of the things he learns in a badly taught course, but those things can be taught separately. The student can be taught how to study and how to think. I don't see any point in making education chaotic and difficult in order to teach the student to rise above a difficult environment. If you want to teach him to rise above a difficult environment, then program a difficult environment.

EVANS: Incidentally, the way teaching machines

have been so well accepted in industry yet so strongly resisted in *educational* institutions illustrates the traditional resistance to innovation in the educational system. In fact, we have explored this phenomenon in a recent book (11). We found in our study of ten universities that even though some professors as individual consultants were instrumental in adoptions by industry of innovations such as programmed instruction, professors in general resisted this in their universities. In fact, we even noted that there was little or no programming for instructional innovations in universities.

SKINNER: Yes, programming is being used widely in industry, because in industry there is an immediate dollars-and-cents value attached to efficient instruction. A company that spends 25 million dollars per year on the instruction of its employees can save 12½ million dollars a year by cutting teaching time in half. Anyone who can save his company 12½ million dollars a year is going to do so. Most of the people now working in the field of auto-instructional methods are being supported by industry. There is no one in a comparable position in education—no one whose job it is to look for more efficient ways of teaching, no one with the authority to say, "Look, we can teach algebra twice as quickly with these machines; let's do it." I'm not sure anyone is even looking for more efficient methods. Administrators are concerned with hiring and firing, with housing, and so on, and teachers are concerned with giving assignments. There is no comparable way in which changes in method can be implemented in our educational system. It's a shocking thing, because if we need to cut instructional time in half in industry, there is much greater urgency for cutting it in half in our educational system.

EVANS: Some branches of the Armed Forces are using auto-instructional methods at an increasing level. The Air Force in particular is doing a great amount of training with this method, is it not?

SKINNER: Yes. There again, you have people who are in a position to make decisions. There is no one within the educational system who is in such a position, and unfortunately, those who are on the outside advocating changes are not aware of the possibilities. When we eventually look back on educational reform in the 1960's, we will see that those who have spoken out most vigorously have completely neglected method.

EVANS: Incidentally, Dr. Skinner, here in your own work environment, have you applied some of your own principles of management of the environment?

SKINNER: Yes. Contrary to what my critics have said, I regard myself simply as an organism responding to its environment. This is my environment. It's designed to bring out my verbal behavior with maximal efficiency.

EVANS: Getting back to the criticisms of these methods, some of those who have resisted the use of teaching machines have maintained that shaping behavior in this manner is detrimental to the development of individuality, and contrary to the spirit of democracy. Do you see the possibility of controlling behavior in a manner consistent with your principles without doing violence to individuality?

SKINNER: Rousseau, whose book *Émile* (37) is

really a great treatise on education, was a champion
of the rights of man. But at one point, he slips. He
says something like this: "You will teach your student
as he wants to be taught, but never forget that it is
within your power to make him want what you want
him to want." And this is true, whether we admit it or
not. The humanist who uses persuasion, argument,
inducement, emulation, or enthusiasm to get a student to learn is controlling the student just as defi-
nitely as the person who designs a program or a teaching machine. If the student arrives at the same end
point, then the question is merely one of means to that
end. The fact is that techniques of teaching based on a
traditional conception of the human organism don't
work well. They have been in use for two or three
thousand years, and haven't proved very effective.
Something else must be tried.

EVANS: You are introducing here some pertinent
questions relevant to educational philosophy in general. In American education there has been a continuing struggle over the concepts of "content" versus
"method." The importance of this distinction is indicated when a layman like Admiral Rickover can
have such sweeping effect on significant decision-
makers in our society by announcing that we should
move away from our over-preoccupation with method
and concern for the individual. He groups "method"
and the John Dewey–type humanism together as
"evils." He argues that the teacher must decide what
is good for the student, and present it to the student
with little concern for the needs of the student as an
individual learner. That's the method basically used

for two thousand years, as you said, and I wonder what you think about this notion.

SKINNER: I don't think Rickover has a point at all. He says, "I judge an educational system in terms of its products." He prefers the Swiss and English schools to ours, but has he never stopped to think that the Swiss have not produced many creative people or that England is in a real bind because its educational system isn't working either? The British don't know what to do about the eleven-plus program, and their advanced education is strangled by tradition. They produce many distinguished people, but they are not making the best use of the genetic endowment of their population as a whole. The American system may not produce people whom Rickover can hire without further education in building atomic submarines, but it does have a good deal to say for itself. Rickover has no suggestions for improvement. We can copy Swiss and English schools—make sure our children are reading certain materials by a certain grade, but that is really no proposal at all.

EVANS: So, as far as you can see, then, Rickover is advocating a system which hasn't proved too effective either throughout history or in the present.

SKINNER: The whole thing is a question of method. That's the crux of my argument with Carl Rogers; I'd like people to be approximately as Rogers wants them to be. I want independent people, and by that I mean people who don't have to be told when to act or who don't do things just because they've been told they're the right things to do. But how do you build independence? I'm convinced that I can specify methods which will be more effective than Rogers'. I just don't think his conception of inner determiners is valid. We agree on our goals; we each want people to be free of the control exercised by others—free of the education they have had, so that they profit by it but are not bound by it, and so on. This is all part of the educational design which I'm trying to implement, not only with teaching machines but with the application of an experimental analysis to classroom management. It boils down to a question of method, not of the ultimate worth of the individual. I want to preserve the dignity and worth of a man, too.

EVANS: Your contribution to this issue certainly doesn't follow along any traditional polarities, particularly the ones often plaguing colleges of education. The advocacy of teaching "method" without "content" has come to roost on the back doors of these colleges, and has caused a great deal of hostility toward them, particularly those supporters of a content-centered curriculum who sarcastically suggest that "pooled ignorance doesn't equal knowledge," regardless of the method. I'm sure you've heard this kind of talk.

SKINNER: I would defend our educational system, and John Dewey's ideas as well. American schools are suffering from undersupport and overpopulation, and they haven't solved all their problems, but they are turning out a lot of productive people. They are better than schools of fifty years ago, which couldn't have solved current problems as well, but there is still room for improvement.

EVANS: The individuality you refer to here would

be something different from the products of a completely mechanistic system, then, and certainly not the image conjured up by critics of your approach. You seem to be advocating the overall values of a good life, and you certainly point to an individual's independence of action.

SKINNER: I don't say that the individual will be completely free; he can never be that. He can become free of objectionable kinds of control.

EVANS: But to go back to a point we discussed earlier: you suggested that it would be an oversimplification to describe man as a "machine."

SKINNER: Oh, of course. I don't think it is necessary to use a mechanistic analogy here. But as an example of what I mean, take a child whose family has a lot of trouble getting him off to school on time. The bus is going to be at the corner in a few minutes and the child is just finishing his breakfast. Now his parents are tempted to say, "Come on, get your coat on. Get your coat on. Hurry up, it's time for the bus," and so on. They may do that for years, because the child will wait for this verbal stimulus before getting his coat on and going out to the school bus. But what is wanted is a child who will put his coat on without being told, who responds to the clock on the wall, to the progress of breakfast, or to other stimuli correlated with time. We want him to come under the control of his environment rather than of verbal directions given by members of his family. The child who is able to get through breakfast and get his coat on and meet the bus day after day on his own without being told is in a sense free. He is still controlled by his environment but he is free of the control of his mother's voice. That's a big difference. It's an important one because of the implications for personal maturity.

EVANS: We've looked at several areas now, where your principles of behavior can be applied to improve efficiency and effectiveness in education, but we have not specifically discussed your philosophy of education. First of all, I wonder how you feel your learning-teaching model can be integrated into the system as it stands, to make it more effective.

SKINNER: As I suggested earlier, I think educators have .done a very good job, given the resources at their disposal and the attitudes of the public toward them. But they can do much more. Teaching machines are only one aspect of a whole technology of teaching. I've done a book on that subject (49) but it is not about teaching machines any more than Ferster's and my book (12) was about the equipment we used to arrange schedules. Devices of many kinds will certainly be used—and for very good reasons. One is to get away from aversive control. There is an article in this morning's paper saying that teachers in New York are no longer going to be allowed to assign homework as punishment. Schoolwork is considered *punishment*. You'll find teachers who excuse students from schoolwork as a *reward*. That's just the wrong way around. Additional homework ought to be rewarding, and if you want to punish someone, you should deprive him of the opportunity to study. But this is as unthinkable as using positive reinforcement to control traffic violations. We are committed to a punitive system, and we are experiencing all the by-products of it: dropouts, truants, vandalism, and so on. But to effect a change you've got to arrange much better schedules of reinforcement than the teacher can possibly arrange when working with a large group of students. If you had an individual tutor for each student, it's conceivable that standard methods could be appropriately employed. But you don't, and so you have to work out other ways in which the student will be appropriately reinforced to shape his behavior progressively toward the goals of education. A technology of teaching should emphasize individual instruction. Educators pay lip service to that; they advocate individual instruction. But their practices are as regimented as they can possibly be. A state board specifies exactly what the student should be studying all the way through the system. Nothing could be more regimented than that, but we know they aren't going to learn what is specified and so we're not worried. We now solve the problem of regimentation by teaching badly. With proper instrumentation, and with a system based on proper methods, it should be possible to allow the individual to follow his own bent and to work at his own speed. The good student could move quickly, and the slow student, who is not necessarily unintelligent, could work at his own effective pace.

EVANS: Of course, there is an attempt to do just this in systems where students are grouped according to levels of ability.

SKINNER: Oh, yes. The track system, special classes for bright students, and so on, are efforts to solve the problem. But they aren't solutions, because even

among bright students some will move faster than
others. You can't fragment a school completely for
administrative reasons. With proper instructional materials, however, a student in a small country school
could pursue a special course of study effectively.

The way to avoid aversive control is to maximize
positive reinforcement. Other benefits follow. We now
teach subject matters: geography, arithmetic, spelling,
grammar, and so on—in other words, various reperto-
ries of responses. Indirectly we teach what we call
abilities: ways of thinking, ways of solving problems.
Those can be attacked directly and taught much more
effectively. I predict that the curriculum of the future
will be designed around various capacities and abilities rather than around subjects. It is much more
important to teach clear thinking, ways of memorizing, or thinking in three dimensions, than geography,
history, or mathematics.

EVANS: If some educational psychologists heard
you describe it this way, they might observe, "Well,
this sounds a little bit like the old discarded idea of
mental discipline."

SKINNER: I don't believe in mental discipline as
such, but I certainly believe that something happens
when, let us say, you memorize a poem or facts of
geography. Techniques of memorizing are common to
both and, as special skills, could be taught by themselves, apart from subject matter. Then you could turn
the student over to a subject matter, and he would get
it more quickly. But I'm much more concerned with
the student's so-called personality traits—his interest
in what he's doing, his perseverance, his ability to

stick with an unpleasant task, his enjoyment of literature—things like that. It is difficult in the present system to teach a student to read for mere enjoyment.
The wrong contingencies are at work. Most schools
are proud of what their students are reading: "Oh,
well, but in the tenth grade we teach Dostoevski."
They probably do, but how many students are reinforced when reading Dostoevski at that age and
continue to read because they are? It's a serious
question. By scheduling reading material so that the
student is reinforced at the right time, we can "hook"
him so that he will go on reading more and more
difficult things and continue to read throughout his
life. We shouldn't teach great books; we should teach
a love of reading. Knowing the contents of a few
works of literature is a trivial achievement. Being inclined to go on reading is a great achievement.

EVANS: In an attempt to validate these theories,
would you recommend a radical experimental reorganization of a specific institution, or would you prefer
to institute these reforms more gradually into various
existing educational systems?

SKINNER: The problem of implementation is prodi-
gious. I hate to think of the administrative changes
required to improve education as we know it could be
improved. Change will come slowly. It is not too hard
for teachers to use programmed materials as adjuncts
to other kinds of teaching, but this won't solve the
problem in the long run. You want the individual student to move ahead at his own rate, but if every student were really allowed to do so, the confusion
would be fantastic. Yet the problem must be solved.

We simply must not hold back quick students or force slow students to go so fast that they miss important steps and hence go still slower and eventually become hopelessly discouraged.

EVANS: Dr. Skinner, perhaps it might be interesting at this point to examine a typical concrete example of difficulties that plague the teacher in the present system to illustrate how you would analyze it. For example, many students appear to develop a mental block in mathematics. What do you see as the cause for a block of this sort? What in the system can be responsible for it?

SKINNER: Of course, a mental block is a fiction— we must understand that first. You can't operate on a student like a surgeon to cut out a mental block. But you can improve the programming. I wouldn't presume to predict how far every student could go in mathematics when properly programmed, but I'm sure it would be much farther than is now the case.

EVANS: This leads us into a somewhat related area which has become important to contemporary writers who have criticized our educational system and general cultural climate from a different perspective. They introduce the notion that we have become a society of overconformists. For example, David Riesman discussed it in *The Lonely Crowd* (35). Do you feel it's a meaningful statement to say that man is overconforming?

SKINNER: I think man could be much less conforming than he is. Our school systems could bring people even more under the control of the natural environment and less under the control of "what other people say," what they read, what they memorize by way of rituals which control their daily life. I'm all for that. But that would raise problems on its own; a world in which people were freely and wildly original could be a very difficult world to live in, too. A certain amount of conformity is needed for just the ordinary articulation of a group. I don't feel, personally, that it is particularly valuable to ride the issue of conformity in defining a better world. Nonconformity is not what you want, any more than conformity. You want people who are making the most of themselves, and this usually means people who are least under the control of manners, customs, and other people. I seldom think in terms of conformity; I don't think it's a useful concept.

EVANS: It's interesting to hear you voice your unconcern for this concept, since it has come to be an issue in some quarters. Incidentally, Ernest Jones (6) made an interesting remark about the notion of overconformity, when he said that the fact that we're so preoccupied with the idea is a good sign we're not actually overconforming. This is an interesting way of putting it.

SKINNER: Yes. I doubt whether a really conforming population would ever raise such a question.

EVANS: Another issue which seems to emerge out of this discussion of our educational system is the question of the changing role of the American woman. There has been a lot of discussion about the matter, and in fact, there seem to be more and more women past thirty-five returning to school in order to get more meaning in their life. Do you have any comments to make on this subject?

SKINNER: I don't have any very strong feelings

about it one way or the other. As a citizen, not a
psychologist, I feel sorry that women in our culture do
not find activities which are of greater interest. I
don't know whether there is any basic reason they do
not contribute more to public life, to the arts, and so
on. It is easy to attribute it to a basic difference or to
cultural preoccupations which keep them busy with
other things. But that is out of my range. I have no
way of finding out whether women generally are
brighter in one area and duller in another, or whether
it is all due to cultural factors. I have nothing to say
about this, and had better stop right here.

ISSUES IN CONTEMPORARY PSYCHOLOGY

CHAPTER 4

Overview | In this chapter we discuss some of the issues which face psychology today. For example, should the psychologist be most concerned with a basic research-oriented approach, or should he, if he can, direct himself toward solving problems in society, without sacrificing his scientific balance?

Professor Skinner wrote a provocative article which has been interpreted as suggesting that theories as such may not be necessary in psychology. Here, he expresses what his feelings actually are concerning the value of theory.

Skinner's views concerning the appropriate training for psychologists are also elicited. Skinner discusses some innovative notions. He also presents some interesting views concerning creativity and whether or not he believes creativity can be taught. Finally, he presents his strong reservations concerning training in statistics and experimental design—both of which are virtually "sacred cows" in current training in the behavioral sciences.

EVANS: Dr. Skinner, one issue of increasing importance on the contemporary scene is the challenge to psychology to solve human problems. For example, the war on poverty or the problems of civil rights, mental retardation and mental illness present challenges to our profession by government at a level greater than ever before in history. Still the most scientifically prestigious manner for a psychologist to operate would appear to be to work in his isolated laboratories engaging in basic animal research. How do you feel about this question: should a psychologist seek acceptance by the scientific establishment of our profession, and achieve a rather comfortable existence by studying animals and doing fairly basic research; or should he become involved in attempting to solve applied problems of immediate significance to our society?

SKINNER: He can be both, or be either one separately. This should be left up to the individual. Human behavior and animal behavior are extremely complex subjects. You can no longer deal with them with a few general principles. We need a lot of dedicated people who love nothing more than going into the laboratory and spending a lifetime in research. I've seen many of my students do that kind of thing. It's fascinating. They make progress, and the methods pay off. There are always interesting things turning up in animal research, and I wouldn't want to suggest that these people should shift their orientation. On the other hand, I always point out to my students the implications of this kind of work, because I feel they should know what they are really doing, and see what it all amounts to. I often question students after they've reported on an experiment: Have you looked for parallels in real life? Often they haven't, but there usually are important parallels, and what a man has just reported may have terrific implications.

But I'm not disturbed at all by the narrow student who will go along all his life happily investigating specific problems under rigorous laboratory control. On the other hand, I am just as anxious to encourage a student who has acquired his spurs through laboratory research to turn to matters which are important for society in general. I'm very much impressed by work with exceptional children, psychotics, retardates, and so on, in which the scientist brings to bear on the problem special techniques acquired under more rigorous conditions. There's enough reinforcement for a man working in that area to last him a lifetime. I've done both. I've enjoyed my laboratory work, and I went for years without bothering to look at its implications. In fact, I was so unconcerned with extrapolations at that time that I even wrote, in *The Behavior of Organisms* (40), "Let him extrapolate who will." Now, of course, I extrapolate all the time.

EVANS: This book came out in 1938, so your views have changed some since then, have they not?

SKINNER: That's right. I was still a young man, and I was still dedicated to and reinforced by what was happening in the laboratory. That was enough for me. It would still be enough for me, except that I have come to see that my laboratory work bears on many other things which have interested me over the years. Nowadays my work is at the other end of the continuum. I no longer even have a laboratory. Other people have taken over that sort of thing and are doing magnificent work. I'm glad I'm getting out, because I can't understand what they are doing these days. I've turned, instead, to fields which seem to me to be extremely important and to which a basic analysis brings something which cannot be found anywhere else.

EVANS: We've spoken about the scientific establishment in psychology, and while I'm not too sure that there is such an establishment, there does seem to be a developing consciousness of research-oriented as against practicing psychologists. Do you feel that these two points of view are growing further apart?

SKINNER: There certainly is a clear distinction between the profession of psychology as practiced by the clinician and the applied psychologist, and laboratory science practiced by the researcher. They should be in close contact with one another, and I've done what I could to establish contact between them. The pure scientist gets swamped sometimes because there are so many more professional psychologists than experimental. The researchers in the American Psychological Association are far from the majority, and we are in danger of getting lost. It seems to me some reorganization of the Association is needed to allow for recognition and identification of smaller groups. Just bringing people together physically helps to maintain the identity of a group, but unless you look around carefully at an APA meeting, you don't see anybody you know, and that's not good. A new division for members interested in the experimental analysis of behavior has helped immensely. We now have a place to meet where we can talk to one another. We have a flourishing journal, and will soon have another. Actually, the kind of thing I'm interested in is expanding very rapidly. At a recent meeting of the APA, eight different companies displayed equipment used primarily in operant research. Unfortunately, much of it is elaborate and expensive, but it encourages good work. Hundreds of laboratories in America are now using operant-conditioning techniques, and there are a good many abroad also. I don't think that as behaviorists we need feel that our identity is in any sense threatened.

EVANS: Is this new division a meeting ground for both applied and basic researchers, where there is mutual acceptance and both are equal in prestige?

SKINNER: It's a division[1] based on methodology

[1] At this time the American Psychological Association, with membership numbering well over 20,000, consists of twenty-six

and an area of research. Before it was established, we held annual conferences for twenty years, eventually within the APA, but we couldn't get sufficient space. Now we have our own division, we can schedule our own programs and get space enough for the people interested in attending them. This isn't empire building. Empire building doesn't interest me in the slightest . . . it's just a matter of finding the time and place for the easy exchange of information. The new division allows for such an exchange, and I am satisfied.

EVANS: Delving a little further into the role of psychologists, you are saying that applied psychology, so long as it is based in sound theory, contributes a great deal to the science, but there are some within the applied field who may be dealing with highly specific areas with little generalizing of results possible, such as building systems and doing research for various agencies such as the Department of Defense. How do you feel about this trend?

SKINNER: I'm not sure such research involves them as psychologists. I'm not at all impressed by the model builders, the information theory analysts, the systems analysts, and so on. They still haven't shown me that they can do anything important. Many of them seem to be looking for an alternative to an empirical science, and I don't believe there is any such thing. Some of them are outright formalists, but formalism has been tried elsewhere, as in linguistics,

divisions which reflect the various interests of members. The division to which Dr. Skinner refers here is the Division of Experimental Analysis of Behavior (Division 25).

without much success. I don't look for much help
from these people; the learning theorists who set up
mathematical models don't keep up with the data, or
they generate data using large groups of subjects.
They aren't contributing anything we can use, and in
fact, what they are doing usually seems rather ludi-
crous. It's not psychology; it's not an empirical science.
It scares me to think that the Pentagon hires these
people to decide whether or not to push the button. I
don't think decisions that are worth anything can be
made that way.

EVANS: This is interesting, since there are some
who would say that the use of elaborate programming
involved in choice-making decisions is similar to the
auto-instructional methods you've described in your
own work. I gather, then, that you do not feel there
is any similarity between the two kinds of programming activities?

SKINNER: No, I don't. Programming a computer
and programming instruction are very different
things. I'm interested in analyzing behavior. There
are others—many in the field of decision-making—who
confine themselves to analyzing the contingencies of
reinforcement to which behavior is submitted. An
analysis of the contingency is not a substitute for a
study of the way in which the organism responds to
contingencies. I don't see any way of avoiding the
effort involved in an empirical analysis of behavior.
You can't sit down "at the green table" and generate
theories which circumvent empirical research. It
doesn't work in physics, and it doesn't work in psychology.

EVANS: You're saying, then, that the role of the psychologist should be an empirical one; that once he becomes concerned with broad-scale human problems he should maintain his empirical orientation?

SKINNER: Yes. I'm all for practical problems; I think you learn a lot from them. During the Second World War we faced a practical problem in getting pigeons to guide missiles. We had to control the behavior of the pigeon beyond the shadow of a doubt, and in order to do that we had to examine every variable conceivably related to its behavior. Laboratory research usually doesn't require this degree of certainty; you can let the effects of some variables average out over a period of time, or at least you don't have to guarantee the degree of precision needed in our project. That experience was profitable because it led to an entirely different conception of the determination of behavior. It also provided an opportunity to test practical applications of basic research, and we were pleased to see that we could produce a very complex performance successfully.

EVANS: Aside from being an example of scientifically profitable spin-offs from mission-directed research, your demonstration of pigeon-guided missiles was a very creative and ingenious enterprise. Yet, for some reason or another, this demonstration did not meet with a strong reception, and your idea was apparently not adopted. This leads to the consideration of another very important issue in teaching, that of the encouragement and development of creativity, particularly in a culture where it often fails to be reinforced. As you know, psychologists are becoming more concerned about the problem of creativity training. So far, however, the payoff in this area has been incredibly small. How do you feel about creativity and the possibilities of teaching individuals to be more creative?

SKINNER: It's an interesting problem to a determinist, because, to him, nothing can be truly creative. It is also an interesting problem in the analysis of teaching, because, by definition, you cannot teach creative behavior. If it's creative, it has not been taught. But there are ways in which one arrives at behavior which is less stereotyped or routine or, to all intents and purposes, original. Even though a science of behavior views the individual as a determined system, it clearly recognizes his uniqueness. Every one of us is a unique combination of genetic and environmental variables—the locus through which these variables come to fruition in behavior. Many people become depressed when they are convinced that they are not capable of a spontaneous change of course, but they usually recover when they realize how unique they are. Now, if you want a scientist to do original research, not in the sense of something originated from nothing, but unique work which only he could do, then you must teach him a scientific method which minimizes routine, standard, everyday humdrum products. If I were to try to isolate the events in my own behavior which have led to original behavior, I would look for them in certain techniques of self-management. Actually, some of my so-called achievements came as the result of rather extraordinary accidents. I have sketched the story in an article, "A

Case History in Scientific Method" (46). If there was anything about my behavior which increased the probability of my profiting from those accidents it was, I think, something in the nature of remaining open to new possibilities. I am very stubborn in adhering to the principle of uniformity in nature, and when an organism does something I think it should not have done, I don't dismiss it as caprice or free will—I try to find out why.

EVANS: This is a very interesting way of looking at the notion of creativity. But going back to the example of the way society reacted to your proposed use of pigeons for a task one ordinarily would expect a man to carry out, it was an indication of the reluctance we often see to accept creativity when it emerges, particularly when it represents something incongruent with existing "sets." Why do you think it is that society seems to encourage creativity in one context, but rejects it in another?

SKINNER: I'm not sure we do very much by way of encouraging creativity. The important creative steps which mean something to people are, of course, applauded; we don't know how to encourage creativity except to applaud it when it occurs. But although people are prepared to accept a certain kind of novelty, and reinforce the men who achieve it, they are usually not prepared to accept, and in fact are disturbed by, anything which is very different. That was our problem with the engineers in the missile project —no one would take us seriously. They didn't know there was a science of behavior. They didn't realize that an organism such as a pigeon could be accurately controlled, and they wouldn't entrust it with an expensive piece of equipment. The possibility was out of their field entirely. They were simply not ready to believe in the reliability of a living thing, even though it was true (and is still true) that an organism of that kind can do things which no known machine can do and even though, in fact, the pigeons were far more reliable than the missiles.

EVANS: Our discussion thus far has led us to the brink of another important issue in psychology: the question of theory building as opposed to developing a paradigm or model. How do you feel about this?

SKINNER: It depends on what you mean by theory. I have been called an antitheorist, probably because of a paper I wrote entitled, "Are Learning Theories Necessary?" (42), even though I carefully defined what I meant by theory. I defined theory as an effort to explain behavior in terms of something going on in another universe, such as the mind or the nervous system. Theories of that sort I do not believe are essential or helpful. Besides, they are dangerous; they cause all kinds of trouble. But I look forward to an overall theory of human behavior which will bring together a lot of facts and express them in a more general way. That kind of theory I would be very much interested in promoting, and I consider myself to be a theoretician. I am working on a book which I will probably call "Contingencies of Reinforcement" but which might as well be called "A Theoretical Analysis of Behavior."

I don't accept most current analyses of scientific methodology, however, or statistical methods which are taught as if they were the way scientists think. In general, scientific methodology is not an accurate reflection of what the scientist really does. It's a mistake to teach students to "begin with a problem, work out a hypothesis, deduce a theorem, design an experiment to test the theorem, and confirm or disprove the hypothesis." This is an a posteriori reconstruction of what happens, and it doesn't reflect the actual behavior of the scientist. Fortunately for science, scientific method and statistics weren't formulated until the middle of the nineteenth century. Science had got a good start before scientists were told what they ought to be doing. I certainly don't feel that my own scientific activities are adequately described by statistics or scientific method or model building.

EVANS: When you refer to the differences in theory as opposed to model building, the question of training of students arises. We continue to teach students to use a hypothetico-deductive[1] orientation, and there seems to be a great deal of importance placed on it. You seem to be saying, then, that the area of experimental design is not too important an element in the training of students, are you not?

SKINNER: I prefer to bring my students into contact with subject matter as quickly as possible, and show them how to spot useful lines of investigation and how to discard useless. No student of mine to my knowledge has ever "designed an experiment." Experimental design is all right for certain very simple

[1] This usually involves stating a hypothesis, and in terms of a careful research design, attempting to prove or disprove the validity of the hypothesis.

manipulations of variables, as in Fisher's work (13, 14); but it is not representative of science in general. Once formulated, such methods must be stretched to fit research to which they aren't adapted, and in the end nothing of interest comes out of it. Give a young psychologist some equipment and a behaving organism, let him explore ways of manipulating behavior, and he won't need formal method. He will soon be discovering things which are quite valuable, and abundantly reinforced for doing so.

EVANS: This leads us to the consideration of another point regarding the training of psychology students, and that is the notion that each learns a particular methodology or set of principles which confines him to a narrow field of investigation. In the training of a young psychologist, how do you feel we should proceed to include, say, literature and history? Do you feel this broader field of knowledge would be of value to him and contribute to his training? Also, how broad should his training in psychology be?

SKINNER: That may prove to be an embarrassing question. I don't know. I confess to being a bigot at the outset, so I'll start from there. I don't think that the Great Books doctrine is valid. I see no reason why every individual must climb the tree of knowledge all the way from the roots. The Greeks made a lot of mistakes. They did some good things, and we honor them for it, but we don't need to think everything through the way they did. We wouldn't expect a physicist to begin with Greek physics, and we shouldn't expect the psychologist to begin with Greek psychology. If an idea has survived unchanged, it only shows how bad it was. It wasn't strong enough to produce a better idea. If I were to design a course for students who did not have to answer someone else's final examinations, who were genuinely interested in understanding human behavior, and who wanted to be effective in dealing with it, I should not bother with ordinary learning theory, for example. I would eliminate most of sensory psychology and I would give them no cognitive psychology whatsoever. I would include very little of mental measurement or testing. My students would never see a memory drum. They would study a bit of perception, but in a different guise.

EVANS: A question which might obviously be raised here, Dr. Skinner, would be to point out that, while you advocate a seemingly radical departure from current trends in education for psychologists, both you and a good many of your students are products of a very broad and liberal education, and you have produced some very creative works. Since, as indicated earlier, we know so little about the development of creative individuals, are we not taking the calculated risk that such creativity would not emerge if we limit the areas of training such as you have suggested here?

SKINNER: Oh, I don't mean that I want a really narrow curriculum. I want students to know some history and some literature. And other sciences. I would much rather see a graduate student in psychology taking a course in physical chemistry than in statistics. The relationships in physical chemistry are much closer to the kind of relationships found in the analysis of behavior. A course in physical chemistry shows the student how to deal with systems of variables. And I would include other sciences, even poetry, music, and art. Why not? You could include some of these in place of learning theory.

EVANS: You're advocating, then, a well-educated man, but not one who is trained in a lot of superfluous matters specific to a narrow field of psychology.

SKINNER: I was referring only to those areas of psychology which seem to me to be superfluous.

EVANS: I would like to explore further your earlier observation concerning the use and misuse of statistics in psychological research. I believe you had suggested that focusing on statistical analyses sometimes results in too little attention given to the behavior of the individual organism.

SKINNER: Oh, yes. We tend to average curves, and if we have a large enough grant, we can average a thousand or ten thousand cases and come out with a nice smooth curve. But the nice smooth curve shows none of the characteristic individuality of the organism you're studying. One of the satisfactions about studying operant behavior is that we can successfully study one organism at a time. If organisms differ, then we look more closely to find out why. The degree of rigor achieved with a single organism is very satisfactory. The curves published in *The Behavior of Organisms* in 1938 wouldn't pass muster today. They were "noisy"; they had all sorts of defects. We've developed better ways to control behavior, but we don't do it by averaging. I could have done that in 1938, but I didn't, and this is one of the reasons why we have learned to control the variables which caused the irregularities in earlier records. It is a matter of sticking with a problem rather than getting rid of it. Statistics is often just a way of dodging problems raised by individual subjects.

But there are other things too. In my own thinking, I try to avoid the kind of fraudulent significance which comes with grandiose terms or profound "principles." Some psychologists seem to need to feel that every experiment they do demands a sweeping reorganization of psychology as a whole. It's not worth publishing unless it has some such significance. But research has its own value, and you don't need to cook up spurious reasons why it's important. Another dangerous trap for people exploring new fields is to conclude that something has value because it resembles an achievement in another field. Freud once came up with a neurological theory of the neuroses. He entertained it for two or three weeks with almost pathological excitement, and then suddenly dropped it. His correspondence with Fliess as interpreted by Jones (22), reveals how he was first attracted by the increased credibility which the neurological theory afforded his widely criticized view of the neuroses. But he was soon willing to recognize that it was the language of neurology in itself, rather than its validity, which had swayed him. In other words, it was a poem written in prestigious words which swept Freud off his feet for a couple of weeks. But Freud had the genius to see it through, and in the end threw it away. Many people can't do that. These are some of the things that I would teach young psychologists about the practice of their science.

EVANS: This brings us back to your earlier remarks concerning serendipity or accidental discovery. What you seemed to be saying was that an accidental discovery is not quite as accidental as it would sometimes appear.

SKINNER: It may be accidental as a specific discovery, but it's no accident that you discover things by continuing to look. Even if you're looking for the wrong thing, that's better than not looking at all. It's better to look for the right thing, of course, but keep in mind that looking is the thing; if you're looking for one thing and find something else, you're in luck.

EVANS: Incidentally, I was rather impressed with one of your local bookstores here in Cambridge. I was browsing through it yesterday and it had a separate section on serendipity. There must be some preoccupation with it here at Harvard.

SKINNER: Walter Cannon popularized the idea, of course, when he was professor of physiology at the Medical School. There was a discussion in *Science* recently about what the word is supposed to mean. I felt the last communication I read on it missed the point a bit. Cannon described it as the art of finding one thing when looking for something else, and that is what it was supposed to mean in the original story about the princesses of Serendip.

EVANS: Another issue of importance to psychology deals with some of the fantastic breakthroughs in other scientific disciplines in the last few years, such as the work being done in biochemistry with deoxyribonucleic acid (DNA), and the implications it has for explaining human life. I wonder how you feel such discoveries will affect the conceptualizations of psychology?

SKINNER: I think comparable breakthroughs are going to happen, and are already happening, in the experimental analysis of behavior. But if you mean what bearing will chemical and biological facts have on a science of behavior, that's a different question. I hope that they will have an important effect, and very soon. As I indicated earlier, I'm not opposed to finding out what's going on inside the organism, and I look forward to the day when physiological facts will help in the scientific analysis of behavior. There is obviously something inside the organism which explains the connection between a history of scheduling and a current performance. If someone can identify that something—say, as some arrangement of molecules—fine! It might even stimulate further interest in behavior, but we have plenty of reason to be interested in behavior as it is. No matter how well the gap is filled, it will still be necessary to deal with behavior at a higher level. The geneticist, after all, will still speak in terms of traits and generations; he won't always be talking in terms of DNA. It will be interesting to learn why rate of responding varies with food deprivation, but meanwhile we will continue to use deprivation to control rate of responding.

EVANS: You were confronted with a question of this sort at a symposium in Houston some time ago, and I don't believe you ever had an opportunity to respond to this point at that time. Michael Scrivin, the philosopher, mentioned something to the effect that a danger of a precise and fine methodology for any science is that it can simply be incorporated by other sciences and it will lose its identity as a unique science. Psychologists are often even eagerly working

hand in hand with other scientists in disciplines such
as neurophysiology, biology, and biochemistry. Is it
possible that the methods of psychology (such as
operant conditioning) will simply be absorbed by
these other sciences?

SKINNER: I don't worry about identity as a behavioral scientist. Some operant researchers have found
a place in practical areas, such as research on drugs,
though many of them have soon returned to an academic environment. Some drug companies have
trained their own people to do the same kind of job,
but if a psychologist is out of a job because of that
training, it doesn't worry me. The method is working;
that's the important thing. If the job can be done by a
technician, then it should be. I can't imagine that a
genuine hematologist is very much upset by the fact
that there may be people taking blood samples who
are not hematologists. It doesn't matter to them, nor
can I imagine that the chemists studying the DNA
molecule feel they are losing their identity because
their work is being used by geneticists.

EVANS: You're saying, then, that as a methodology
develops, it is not important who uses it.

SKINNER: It isn't the person who is important; it's
the method. If the practice of psychology survives,
that's the main objective. It's the same with cultural
practices in general; no one survives as a person.

EVANS: We were discussing earlier your views concerning the application of operant principles in the
economy of the Soviet Union. In another vein, I wonder how you view the state of Soviet psychology in
general, today?

SKINNER: I think Soviet psychology is still suffering from the ideological or political use of ideas. Ray Bauer in discussing *The New Man in Soviet Psychology* (5) tells that story very well. Pavlov was accepted by the early Communists because his work suited their methods; the conditioned reflex was just what they wanted. Men were to be changed by changing the environment. But then, as time passed, they found that Russians weren't particularly changed, and it became embarrassing to hold to the conditioned reflex. Stalin turned to the notion of individual initiative and inner determination, and the conditioned reflex was replaced by a purposive psychology. Even the physiologists moved away from the investigation of behavior. Then, when confidence was restored by the war, Pavlov came back into prominence, and psychology turned back to the study of conditioned behavioral reactions. But the damage had been done, and it is still evident today. The psychology being taught, even in education, is couched in neurological terms, and everyone makes this very clear. A teachers' college director will tell you that he is concerned with the higher nervous activities. At the moment, Russians cannot have an objective science of behavior such as we have in this country, because it would be considered idealistic. They've substituted cybernetics. There is much more activity in cybernetics in Russia than in this country, in part because it permits them to deal with behavior in terms which are neither idealistic nor neurological. The mathematics is a safeguard against any charge that one has gone soft. Cybernetics is a possible way

out of the trap in which the history of the movement
has caught them. They're seriously interested in operant conditioning, however. Most of the work is poor.
I wouldn't give an undergraduate a high grade on an
honors' thesis if he came through with the kind of
research I saw there, but at least they feel it is something to look into.

EVANS: Of course, Russians are inalterably opposed to psychoanalytic theory, which the Freudians
would deny is idealistic. Why do you feel that they
resist this orientation?

SKINNER: Mentalistic or idealistic, the net result
is about the same. A psychiatrist friend of mine and a
Russian psychiatrist toured a mental hospital ward
together discussing cases and treatment. The treatment was all couched in terms of conditioned reflexes, but my psychiatrist friend said that in Freudian
terms the treatment would have been much the same.
As far as I'm concerned, both Freudian theory and
conditioned reflexology are cumbersome and unnecessary explanatory systems.

EVANS: You mentioned earlier that you are not
too familiar with conditions in China. Have you had
any opportunity to learn whether or not there is much
interest in psychology in China?

SKINNER: No, but I'm trying now to arrange to go
and find out. They are interested in using teaching
machines, I understand. I'd also like to visit the com-
munes. They are apparently still thriving in spite of
reports to the contrary. But I don't suppose that a
tradition of psychology has survived their great dis-
ruptive wars and revolutions, any more than one has

survived in England, Germany, or France. There is very little continuity between postwar and prewar worlds in psychology, and I would be very much surprised to find any psychology in China that we would recognize as such.

RETROSPECT AND PROSPECT

CHAPTER 5

Overview | To many observers Professor Skinner is emerging as one of the most important and influential scientists in the history of psychology. In this section he has an opportunity to discuss informally what he considers to be the highlights of his illustrious career.

He also discusses some of the ways in which he feels his approach has been misinterpreted. Particularly interesting here is his reaction to the accusation that he in effect has become a protagonist for a point of view which is based on the demonstrated power of positive control.

Perhaps one of the most persistent criticisms of Skinner's contribution is the fact that it is considered by some to be a system which dehumanizes the individual. In this chapter Skinner reacts to his critics on this score.

Finally, he discusses how he envisions the role of psychology both in the present and in the future in the affairs of the world.

EVANS: Dr. Skinner, of all the many intriguing and provocative contributions you have made to the field of psychology, many of which we have touched on in our discussion, which do you feel to be the most significant?

SKINNER: Let me preface my answer by saying that I have had a lot of luck in my scientific career. As I look back on it, it seems to me that two important things were the use of rate of responding as a basic datum and the so-called cumulative record which makes changes in rate conspicuous. Better ways of analyzing rates are coming along now—for example, ways of analyzing inter-response times and computer processing—but even so a cumulative record makes visible at a glance changes in rate of responding over long periods of time. It permits an instantaneous analysis of behavior as an experiment proceeds.

EVANS: It might be interesting to note how you use the clock on the wall here in your study as a means of evaluating your own productivity.

SKINNER: The clock runs when I'm *really* thinking. I keep a cumulative record of serious time at my desk. The clock starts when I turn on the desk light, and whenever it passes twelve hours, I plot a point on a curve. My record begins many years ago. I can see what my average rate has been at any period. When other activities take up my time, like lecturing, the slope falls off. That helps me refuse invitations.

EVANS: I hope that you feel this discussion of ours will be sufficiently valuable that it will compensate for the loss of time on the cumulative record.

SKINNER: I'm sure it will. But to get back to other organisms—once you have rate of responding as a dependent variable you can begin to look for variables which influence that rate. I began in the field of motivation—deprivation and satiation—but I quickly moved into conditioning, contingencies of reinforcement, stimulus control, and so on. As time has passed, of course, records have become smoother and smoother, as we have gained control over more and more variables. This is the heart of the experimental analysis of behavior. Hundreds of people are now engaged in this type of research. It happens to be a method which has worked well. It's producing a corpus of data, a body of knowledge, which is expanding very rapidly. With this method, you're not disproving a hypothesis which you then must discard; you are building on the past, adding details to a picture of behavior as a function of complex contingencies. So far as a laboratory science goes, the picture is a very heartening one.

I have also been interested in extrapolations to other areas. I distinguish between prediction and control as a laboratory enterprise on the one hand, and interpretation on the other. In the latter you make plausible guesses at the variables which are probably operating in a given case—in verbal behavior, say, as in my book (47), or in the contingencies of legal systems. A law specifies behavior and usually some form of punishment. Laws are statements of contingencies backed up by the political systems of the country. Economics is full of tricky schedules of reinforcement—hourly wages, piecework pay, incentive wages—all of which have been beautifully duplicated in laboratory research. Such an application was not what prompted the study of schedules of reinforcement in lower organisms, but the results are certainly relevant to the analysis, not only of incentive systems but of other economic processes. They apply also to the tricky contingencies which arise when people play games. I've analyzed some of the contingencies involved in religious control, and, of course, we've already mentioned psychotherapy. The same analysis applies to ethnic groups and family structures. I've become interested in what I privately term "paleobehavior," the evolution of the behavior of civilized man over hundreds of thousands of years. On the surface it seems to be a kind of accidental programming of very subtle contingencies. When behavior is established it is transmitted to other members. Paleobehavior is almost entirely guesswork, but it is a lot of fun.

EVANS: Having reflected briefly on what you feel

to be some of your significant contributions, Dr. Skinner, would you care to comment here on any particular issue which has been a source of concern to you, perhaps some misinterpretations of your work?

SKINNER: I don't think "concern" would be the right word. I don't expect very many people to be aware of my work or make much use of it until it's had time to grow naturally, and I wouldn't want it to be applied indiscriminately to any and all situations. I don't believe that many psychotherapists, for example, will feel the need to acquaint themselves with the potentialities of positive reinforcement, and it wouldn't be appropriate for them to attempt to apply merely general principles. That would be like building a bridge in terms of general principles of stress and strain. There may arise a new species of therapist who will understand these behavioral mechanisms, but it doesn't bother me that thousands of clinical psychologists don't know the first thing about them. It does bother me that thousands of teachers don't understand, because immediate gains are more likely in the classroom than in the clinic. Teachers will eventually know—they must—and I am far more concerned with promoting my theories in education. There is some interest in the analysis of behavior in political science and economics, but I'm not particularly interested in promoting it there either. I don't complain about the speed with which the science has grown, because it has grown at a pace which maintains its solidity. People at times have charged this kind of analysis with various ignominious shortcomings, saying that somehow it reduced the dignity and nobility of man. But no analysis changes man; he is what he is. I take an optimistic view. Man can control his future even though his behavior is wholly determined. It is controlled by the environment, but man is always changing his environment. He builds a world in which his behavior has certain characteristics. He does this because the characteristics are reinforcing to him. He builds a world in which he suffers fewer aversive stimuli and in which he behaves with maximum efficiency. He avoids extremes of temperature; he preserves food to avoid hunger. He builds a world in which he is more likely to get on with his fellowman, in which he is more likely to educate himself so that he will be more effective in the future, and so on. If you want to argue from history, you can say that over a period of, say, a hundred thousand years there has been an accumulation of behavioral techniques which have improved the effectiveness of human behavior. Man controls himself, but he does so by controlling his environment.

EVANS: As you look to the future, Dr. Skinner, do you feel that in this era of the proliferation of nuclear-bomb capability, there is any way to solve the increasingly complex problems we see challenging the hopes for peace in the world—or for that matter, avoiding the destruction of man?

SKINNER: Of course, this isn't the first time we've developed lethal devices, and I feel quite sure that man will survive this one too. He probably will do it by developing a genuine science of his own behavior. I am worried only about problems of implementation. We're pretty well along toward an effective science, but implementation is the next step. I'm very much disturbed by the kinds of opposition one encounters when trying to apply a science of behavior to human betterment. People who genuinely want to help me are taking positions which may prevent the application of behavioral science for a long time to come.

EVANS: There have been some attempts to do so-called "peace research" along this line, but the unfortunate part of it is that the term "peace" often has been perceived as a propaganda symbol rather than a genuine goal to create understanding between nations. Do you feel psychology has something to contribute along this line?

SKINNER: I'm not particularly happy about what psychologists have done so far in this field. I remember, before the Second World War, a petition psychologists were urged to sign on the premise that it would influence people in power. I've forgotten the gist of the thing, but it was rather more wishful thinking than anything psychologists could responsibly support. There have been other efforts recently. Osgood's proposal (33) seems to me valid. It is practical and specific. I don't subscribe to the notion that wars begin in the minds of men; they begin when somebody steps across a border or fires a gun, and none of that is in the mind. If you want to analyze what starts a war, do so, but don't begin by looking into the minds of men. That gets you nowhere. Personally, I don't try to advise anyone, in Washington or elsewhere, about specific problems. Too many variables are involved. One of the tragedies of the Freudian heritage is that it has encouraged psychologists to try to answer all sorts of questions. "Why did Hamlet hesitate about murdering his uncle?" A sensible man would say, "I haven't the slightest idea," but the psychologist starts answering the question before it has been finished. Plausible explanations cannot be given on the strength of a small fraction of one percent of the relevant evidence. Before I could answer any question about a practical political situation, I should have to spend a few years finding out what is going on, and probably then wouldn't know enough to apply principles of behavior directly to that situation. It might be possible to draw up what might be called a thermodynamics of international policy, which would provide some guidance. If you are faced with two courses of action, check off all possible foreseeable consequences before making a choice. I don't like to make specific recommendations, but we have often mistakenly supported individual rulers when we might better have supported practices we believe in. I should like to see our government set up a large educational agency in which specialists could be sent to train teachers in foreign countries on their invitation, leaving as soon as the job is done. Then you could say to a country, "We don't care who is in power; but if you want the people in your country to be educated, we will build schools, we will staff them temporarily, educate teachers as quickly as possible, and then get out." Regardless of political philosophy, it's better for us that the people of a country be literate. The same thing could be done in the areas of health, birth control, and other programs, by supporting technological programs independent of local governments. Of course, if the governments don't want outside help, that's that.

EVANS: To conclude our "dialogue," it might be interesting to return to a discussion of reactions to your work. Do you feel that attitudes toward your work have generally undergone some kind of change, one which you may have felt either more pleased or more unhappy about?

SKINNER: For many years I've gone to different universities to lecture, and I usually have the opportunity to speak to both faculty and students. In the last five years or so, I have felt a greater degree of understanding. The questions I am asked these days are more pertinent to the real issues, and are no longer attacks. If there is any opposition, either it stays away from the lecture or it has given up. I couldn't possibly ask for a warmer response than I've had recently when talking to university students. It's more profitable for both of us when we get along well, and I always come away feeling that I have learned as much as the students.

EVANS: As you've spoken about culture in these terms, there have been some rather personal indictments of you by people who feel that you are becoming a propagandist for a value system that you would impose on society. How do you feel about these reactions?

SKINNER: I know there are people who are disturbed by this kind of analysis, but I have never felt that it was a personal attack on me. I don't regard myself as a propagandist, if by that you mean using anything except perfectly straightforward ways to promote a subject matter. I don't write argumentative papers, and I don't debate issues with other people. The single exception to this has been with my friend Carl Rogers, with whom I've debated on several occasions on the question of the dignity of man and the ultimate control of men. It doesn't particularly bother me that people should be disturbed, and I'm not out to allay disturbance. My scientific work has been just a report of facts and of what I have found to be effective as formulations. Recently, it is true, I have decided to spend time in clearing up misunderstandings, bringing loose ends together, and so on. I have arrived at a point in my career where I feel I will no longer be making important scientific discoveries, and I've decided to spend more time reading what others have done, and writing primarily to further understanding. I don't regard this as propaganda. I have never attempted to build an empire. I have never set up a Center for Operant Conditioning, for example. I'm quite content with the speed with which the field has moved along. I am particularly happy to see how well people in the field get along with each other. When operant conditioners get together, there is never any criticism or bickering. Everyone tries to be helpful. They practice positive reinforcement, and it is a wonderful thing. It's not that we're wonderful people; it is just that there is plenty for all, and no reason to fight over it. If someone else gets on, it doesn't mean that one's chances of getting on have been injured. It's really quite a luxurious way to live. The methods pay off beautifully. All sorts of things are being discovered, and we're all very friendly and happy. If more people want to come in, that's fine, because there's still more to be done.

EVANS: Well, I think that this certainly gives us an unusual view of your contributions to a science of behavior. Some of these questions were, I am sure, rough for you. I appreciate the fact that you avoided none of them. I must also say, Dr. Skinner, it has been a real pleasure to me personally to be here in your office and workshop, and see the kind of environment in which you, yourself, are positively reinforced. Thank you very much.

SKINNER: Thank you.

The Dialogue Format— An Innovation in Teaching

The dialogue style of presenting the views of the world's outstanding contributors to psychology was designed originally as an innovative teaching device. In 1957 the series was launched with the completion of dialogues with the late Carl Jung and Ernest Jones, supported by a grant from the Fund for the Advancement of Education. It is being continued under a current grant from the National Science Foundation. A basic purpose of the project is to produce for teaching purposes a series of films recording these dialogues which introduce the viewer to our distinguished interviewees' major contributions to the fund of personality psychology and human behavior. It is our hope that these films will also serve as documents of increasing value in the history of the behavioral sciences.[1]

The volumes in this series

APPENDIX 1

[1] The films are distributed by Association Instructional Films, 600 Madison Avenue, New York, N.Y. 10022.

are based on edited transcripts of the dialogue which
include the text of additional audio-taped discussions
as well as the content of the films. It is our hope that
these dialogues in the print medium will extend the
primary goals of the films: (1) to introduce the reader
to the contributor's major ideas and points of view;
(2) to convey through the extemporaneousness of the
dialogue style a feeling for the personality of the contributor.

Since the structure of this volume reflects an innovative approach to teaching, some of our concerns
regarding the proper communication of its intent
might be shared with the reader. When we completed the Jung and Jones book (6), we thought the
word "conversation" could best be used in the title to
describe its process and content. However, we soon
discovered that this seemed to imply to some potential readers of the book something a bit more casual
and superficial than we had intended. While an attempt is made to emphasize spontaneity in our interaction with our participants, since we feel this adds a
dimension to the project that is not usually present in
more didactic forms of teaching, we are hopeful that
this does not detract from any significance that the
content may have. We would hope that a relatively
informal discussion with an outstanding contributor to
a discipline, as he seriously examines his own work,
will not be of less significance by virtue of its informal-
ity.

A more detailed description of the philosophy and
techniques of this project is reported elsewhere (7).
However, a few points bearing on the content of

these volumes might be emphasized. First of all, since the questions are intended to reflect many of the published writings of the interviewee, it might be expected that a comprehensive summary of his work is evoked. However, because of the selectivity necessary in developing the questions so that the discussion can be completed within a limited time interval, it would not be fair to say the results of these sessions—either in the films, which reflect the content emanating from only about half the time spent with the participant, or even in the books, which reflect about twice the amount of time—necessarily provide the basis for an inclusive summary of the contributor's work.

Perhaps more than a comprehensive summary, we are hoping to present a model of a teaching technique which may become an additional means of compensating for the trend observed among many of our students today to become increasingly content with secondary sources to gain information concerning our major contributors in the various disciplines. The material resulting from our dialogues provides a novel "original source" exposure to the ideas of leading contributors to a discipline. Hopefully, this may stimulate the reader to go back to the original writings of the interviewee which develop more fully the ideas presented through our "dialogue." In fact, the term "dialogue" was finally adopted, instead of "conversation," to describe our content and method to imply merely that it represents a programmed teaching effort, in the more traditional Socratic sense. However, the interpretation of the term "dialogue" within the current academic scene often also implies a "challenge" to the individual being "interviewed." Furthermore, to some the term "dialogue" suggests that the questioner is simply using the individual being questioned as a tool to project his own (the questioner's) teaching role into this situation. My own goals here would preclude either of these interpretations of the term "dialogue." It is my intention that these "dialogues" reflect an effort to produce a constructive, novel method of teaching, and cast my interviewer role neither as the center of focus nor as "critical challenger." I would feel that the purpose of this project has been realized if I am perceived as having merely provided a medium through which our distinguished interviewees can express their views. It might be mentioned that our interviewees are generously willing to contribute their time to these efforts in the spirit of the teaching aims of this project. This became evident, for example, in a letter from the late Carl Jung, reproduced in the first chapter of the book based on the Jung and Jones dialogue mentioned earlier. Furthermore, using such sessions as a background for critical examination of the views of the participants might better be left to another type of project, since even if this "critical set" were to be included in my questioning, it might be difficult both to introduce the reader to the contributors' views and to criticize them as well, within our limited time commitment. In fact, I think that some of the individuals who agreed to participate in our project would not have done so if they had sensed that this would become the context for a critical attack on their work.

However, Dr. Skinner was exceedingly forthright in his responses when in the "devil's advocate" role I occasionally presented questions challenging his conceptions which many critics of behaviorism have posited in recent years.

In Appendix II of this volume, I attempt to state some current trends in personality theory which comprise the background against which I formulated the questions used with each of the participants in this project. It seems appropriate to call the reader's attention to one thread which runs through the questions which were developed, namely, the use of Freudian theory as a baseline for them. As a result of my experience in teaching personality theory over the years, I have found that emphasizing the ways in which various theorists agree or differ with traditional Freudian theory becomes a valuable tool for teaching. Of course, the relevance of such an orientation is more apparent in the case of previous subjects of the books in this series, Jung, Fromm, and Erikson. Freudian theory, even as a basis for some of the line of discussion, is much less applicable to B. F. Skinner. However, this orientation is maintained at least peripherally to provide some continuity among the several books in the series.

The present volume is organized in accordance with certain divisions of subject matter which I had planned as I programmed the questions. In the first section my questions are designed to elicit Dr. Skinner's reactions to a number of concepts or areas of focus which have been traditionally generic to the field of psychology in general. The range of these concepts includes Freud's developmental model, the unconscious, motivation and emotions, sensation, perception, and phenomenology—and learning. Learning, of course, includes the constructs most relevant to the development of Skinner's orientation, such as Ivan Pavlov's conditioning paradigm and so-called stimulus-response (S-R) theory in general.

The second section centers on some of Skinner's noteworthy basic contributions. This includes discussions of his impressive case for positive reinforcement and control as against negative reinforcement, punishment, and aversive control. Particular emphasis is placed not only on the theoretical implications of his experimental findings but also on their applications to problems in the world about us. For example, his analysis of the behavior control system in the Soviet Union is most interesting in this respect.

In the third section, Dr. Skinner is asked to examine a number of present-day issues in education and to review his own philosophy of education. The reader will find in this chapter not a wholesale condemnation of our educational system, but an extremely thoughtful evaluation, with highly relevant suggestions for improvements in the learning-teaching system.

The fourth section of this volume focuses on some major contemporary issues in psychology. Here Dr. Skinner answers my questions concerning the relative role of "theoretical" versus "applied" psychology. He is also given an opportunity to discuss graduate training in psychology and to reflect on the relationship of psychology to the other sciences.

The fifth section presents Dr. Skinner's reflections on his own scientific career. It also deals with his analysis of the role of psychologists in helping to solve present and future problems in world affairs. Finally, it offers him an opportunity to respond to some of the critics of his experimental analysis of behavior.

As was the case with subjects of the earlier books in the series (Jung, Fromm, Erikson), it is hoped that the dialogue presentation allows the reader to be introduced to or to reexamine some of Skinner's ideas through a relatively extemporaneous situation, as they are coalesced from the particular point of view inherent in the questions which guide the discussion. It should be pointed out that in his writing, as Skinner expresses himself in his unique style, he has the opportunity to rewrite and to polish until he deems the finished product satisfactory. In the spontaneity of our discussion, however, he is called upon to develop his ideas extemporaneously. I hope that this element of spontaneity may assist in penetrating to the "man behind the book" while losing none of the ideas central to Skinner's thought. Because preservation of this naturalness of communication is essential to the purposes of each volume in this series, few liberties have been taken with the basic content of Skinner's responses to my questions, although some editorial license had to be exercised to shift effectively from oral to printed communication, in the service of accuracy, readability, clarity, and grammatical construction. In fact, Skinner was later given the opportunity to edit and expand answers to some of my questions.

This dialogue as it is presented here duplicates

insofar as possible the tenor of the exchange between
Dr. Skinner and myself as it actually took place. In
spite of some of the editing which was necessary both
in Skinner's responses, as indicated above, and in my
questions, it was a pleasant surprise to review our
hours of discussion and see how few deletions and
alterations were required. We hope that the flow of
material, though extemporaneous, is sufficiently well
organized to make this a worthwhile teaching tool. We
also hope this makes available to the reader some
reactions not readily obtainable from Skinner's traditional didactic presentations.

When confronted with a man like B. F. Skinner,
who so graciously consented to participate in our project, one is tempted to try to gain some notion of what
he is like as a human being. It would be presumptu-
ous, of course, to imply that I could evaluate defini-
tively a man of his complexity on the basis of a few
hours of interaction. Yet, I feel even this limited interaction and subsequent meetings with him provide
me with some insights into the nature of this remark-
able man.

First of all, one cannot help being impressed by
his almost boundless energy, not utilized in mere
random activity, but in carefully planned and directed expenditure of effort. His intellectual breadth
is visible at every turn, not only in areas specifically
indigenous to psychology but in history, art, music,
and literature as well. Readers who are concerned
with his ostensibly mechanistic conceptions of man
may be surprised to learn that Dr. Skinner appears
to me to be essentially a humanist in the most

straightforward connotation of this term. This is evidenced by his concern with eliminating aversive control in society, his optimism concerning man's capability for dealing with his most difficult problems, and his staunch belief in the basic potential of *all* men for a "good life" regardless of their deficits in so-called measured intelligence and their so-called emotional limitations.

In conclusion, I should like to reiterate that in the preceding dialogue the questions presented to Dr. Skinner were designed to allow his views to emerge as coherently yet as spontaneously as possible. In the context of such extemporaneous discussion it is difficult enough to maintain a logical progression without the added distraction of cameras, recorders, film and sound crew members, and others whose presence was necessary during my exchanges with B. F. Skinner. In fairness to him, I must point out that this was a situation far from ideal for him to be expected to produce a polished presentation of his ideas; yet, as pointed out earlier, he was able to organize his thoughts in a most communicative manner. I feel that our objective of an integrated presentation, maintaining the atmosphere of essentially free exchange, was adequately realized. With this view I hope the reader agrees.

The Theoretical Context of the Dialogue

Rather than attempt to summarize all of the major concepts presented in the dialogue as we did in the volumes based on Jung and Fromm, I shall again—as I did in the Erikson volume—take the liberty of briefly presenting frameworks which I find valuable in teaching personality theory to students, hoping they may in turn be of value to the reader of this book in comprehending the backdrop against which we may look at contemporary contributors to psychology such as B. F. Skinner. However, it should be re-emphasized that Professor Skinner is included in this series *not* because he can in any sense be called a "personality psychologist," but rather because he presents historically the most important alternative to a personality psychology. As I indicated in the Appendix I, a few questions based on Freudian theory were asked of Skinner. These were intended merely as a focal point of comparison of

Skinner's views with those of Jung, Fromm, and Erikson, for whom the questions based on Freudian theory were intrinsically more appropriate.

There are three frameworks around which I believe current approaches to personality can be analyzed in order to help to locate any theoretical position within the matrix of general personality theory. These frameworks are really descriptive approaches to the understanding of personality which develop theoretically from basic orientations focusing upon biological determinism, cultural determinism, or self-determinism.

One group of contributors, apparently emphasizing biological determinism, has been considered more or less traditionally psychoanalytical. It includes such writers as Hans Sachs and Ernest Jones, as well as Freud himself. This group has been characterized as emphasizing what Freud called "repetition compulsion," a concept which maintains that the first five years of life, which are strongly influenced by biological propensities, are very important in human development because they set the stage for and determine a life style which is manifested continuously throughout the individual's lifetime; central to this postulate is the notion of the Oedipal complex. Another important aspect of traditional Freudian theory was brought out by Ernest Jones in our earlier published dialogue with him (6), in which he unabashedly makes the statement, "Well, man is, after all, an animal." Some people think that this is a cynical view, although Jones denied that Freud was inordinately cynical. Freud's earliest picture of man is that of an organism dominated to a large degree by its id—the animal, biological side of him—against which the ego—the conscious, the self of man—is fighting a tough battle. He is seen as just barely able to hold his head above water in the struggle to keep from being drowned by the animal he basically is. This view of man, as articulated in Freud's early works, was also accepted by many of the early followers of Freud. With Freud, they believed that the center of man's motivation and energy is the sexual libido, which to them was a manifestation of the dominant animal aspect of man. Although Freud in his later work began to emphasize other aspects of man's makeup also, many thinkers continue to perceive the classical psychoanalytical position in terms of these early views of Freud. Actually, the above description is probably a vast over-simplification of Freud's view, as Fromm (9) and Erikson (10) for example implied in our earlier volumes.

Another group of contributors, the neo-Freudians, has placed more stress on the effects of cultural influences on man's development. To the neo-Freudians, the early Freudians would appear to have taken too seriously the notion that the instinctual animal nature, the repetition compulsion, and a general biological patterning of early development is found *universally* and that these elements dominate man's nature. The neo-Freudians take exception to this concept of universality. They believe that man is primarily a product of the specific kind of culture in which he lives and that learning plays a much more important part than does biological patterning in the development of personality.

The late Karen Horney, for example, a prominent neo-Freudian who had been with the Berlin Psychoanalytic Institute, became so disturbed by many notions in the biological orientation of the early Freudian position, such as the postulation of male superiority (evidenced by the assertion that penis envy was characteristic of women) that she broke away from the orthodox Freudian position. She developed a view (19) that man is shaped to a significant extent by the society with which he must cope when he deals with the anxieties of reality. She considered this anxiety produced by societal pressures more important in shaping man than his anxiety about overcoming his basic biological animal nature.

Again, as indicated in one of our earlier volumes (9), although Fromm does not like the label "neo-Freudian", he too certainly takes exception to Freud's emphasis on the Oedipal situation so central to Freud's "biological unfolding" view of man's development.

Other psychologists have attempted to place man within his social milieu, in the belief that it constitutes the essential force in shaping personality. In spite of the fact that Freud later appeared to be placing more emphasis on the importance of society as a formative influence in the development of individual personality, traditional Freudian theory as it is most often expounded does not emphasize this element. The neo-Freudians made dominant this aspect of man's relationship to his world, emphasizing a cultural determinism which constitutes a departure from what is customarily regarded as traditional Freudian theory. Had Freud emphasized this aspect of the relationship earlier in his writings, he might not have acquired the reputation for being so' biologically oriented. At any rate, many of his immediate followers certainly perpetuated a biological orientation, whereas the neo-Freudians, represented by Horney (19), Abram Kardiner (24), and Harry Stack Sullivan (51), deviated from that point of view. The neo-Freudian group challenged psychoanalysis to extend the study of man at least beyond Freud's early basic tenets.

Another characteristic of the neo-Freudian group is evident in their techniques of psychotherapy. The older Freudians considered psychotherapy a five-day-a-week affair which takes from three to five years of intensive therapy before it can be successful; the neo-Freudians, utilizing recent innovations, believe that situational factors are much more important, and claim to have achieved results with much shorter periods of psychotherapy.

Somewhere between the neo-Freudians and the traditional Freudians there is a group of three significant individuals whom we might describe as Freudian dissentients; for although each of them worked closely with Freud, each subsequently broke with him or was repudiated by him for one reason or another. Carl Jung, Otto Rank, and Alfred Adler would be included in this group.

By all accounts, Adler's early work (1) placed the primary emphasis on the social man, and it might be said that Adler set the stage for the emergence of the neo-Freudian group. In a different direction, although many of his ideas about early biological conceptions were in agreement with Freud's, Rank's preoccupation with the "will" and its development of autonomy introduced a type of self-determinism that Freud apparently did not emphasize.

As became apparent in our dialogue with Carl Jung (6), he had moved away from Freud's basic tenets, while retaining Freud's idea of the unconscious, expanding it into a race and individual unconscious and incorporating into the race unconscious Freud's early notion of archetypes, developing this concept beyond Freud's postulation. However, with this central conception of individuation Jung also moved away from the emphasis on biological determinism. Jung, perhaps more profoundly than either Adler or Rank, turned toward the idea of the development of an ultimately self-determined spiritual being which transcends the biological forces acting on man. This led him to consider many metaphysical conceptions, obviously not in keeping with present-day notions of a scientific psychology.

A great deal of thought today continues to reflect the greater concern for man's individuality and self-responsibility—more than is found in either biological or cultural determinism. For example, the position of the existentialists—particularly in the works of Rollo May (31), the distinguished philosophical theologian Paul Tillich (52), the philosophers Husserl (21) and Heidegger (18), and the work of Carl Rogers (36) in the United States—reflects this concern, as does the work of Abraham Maslow (29) in recent years. Obviously many other psychologists have currently reflected an increased concern with the autonomy of the self, for example Allport (2) and McCurdy (28).

However, it must be kept in mind that related to any theoretical discussion of "determinism" and personality theory, the behavioristic orientation may still be perhaps the most significant theoretical reference group for American academic and research psychologists. As the leading exponent of this view, B. F. Skinner interprets not merely cultural influences in a broad sense, but the immediate environment in a narrow sense as being the significant shaping force on the individual. As environment is controlled experimentally, and even in the clinical situation to modify behavior in a desired direction, very few assumptions concerning the "internal workings" of personality have to be made.

Questions in the dialogue were designed to obtain reactions from Skinner concerning the three orientations described above, but particularly related his views to his particular behavioristic orientation, since it is obvious that to have dwelt in our discussion with Skinner on personality psychology-oriented constructs would have involved an inappropriate level of analysis.

At various points in the dialogue Professor Skinner was given an opportunity to deal directly or indirectly with the differences among the three positions represented by the biological, the cultural, and the self-deterministic points of view. I believe we can say that in his experimental analysis of behavior he has integrated all these three conceptualizations into a purely empirical system, in which generic bases of behavior vis à vis biological, social, or self-determinism are less important than arranging contingencies of reinforcement in the organism's immediate environment, so that the probability of a given response is heightened.

Only within recent years have the experimentally oriented behaviorists come to recognize the need to involve themselves with the issues of immediate concern to society (e.g. 53 and 4). Basic behavior theory has been inclined to develop for what might appear to the outsider to be the exclusive benefit of others interested in behavior theory (e.g., 20). On the current scene, Skinner has been in the forefront in broadening the goals of the experimental analysis of behavior. As some recent reports have emphasized (e.g., 38 and 8), a case can be made for a greater concern with human problems within the province of psychology. The efforts of B. F. Skinner appear to provide provocative baselines for such endeavors, within a rigorous, scientifically acceptable framework.

In conclusion it must be said that aside from anything else he does, B. F. Skinner is one of the great contributors not only to psychology but undoubtedly to a crucial understanding of the greatest challenges to man—the improvement of his educational system and the development of a positive rather than a negative system of shaping the course of life itself.

Bibliography

1. Adler, A. *Understanding Human Nature* (translated by W. B. Wolfe). New York: Greenberg, 1927.
2. Allport, G. W. *Pattern and Growth in Personality*. New York: Holt, Rinehart and Winston, 1961.
3. Ayllon, T. "Intensive Treatment of Psychotic Behavior by Stimulus Satiation and Food Reinforcement." *Behavior Research and Therapy*, 1963, Vol. I, 53–61.
4. Bandura, A., and R. H. Walters. *Social Learning and Personality Development*. New York: Holt, Rinehart and Winston, 1963.
5. Bauer, R. A. *The New Man in Soviet Psychology*. Cambridge: Harvard University Press, 1952.
6. Evans, R. I. *Conversations with Carl Jung and Reactions from Ernest Jones*. New York: D. Van Nostrand Company, 1964.
7. ———. "Filmed Dialogues with Notable Contributors to Psychology." Paper presented at American Psychological Association meetings, Chicago, 1966.
8. ———. "A New Interdisciplinary Dimension in Graduate Psychological Research Training: Dentistry." *The American Psychologist*, 1966, Vol. 21, No. 2, 167–172.
9. ———. *Dialogue with Erich Fromm*. New York: Harper & Row, 1966.
10. ———. *Dialogue with Erik Erikson*. New York: Harper & Row, 1967.
11. Evans, R. I. and P. K. Leppmann. *Resistance to Innovation in Higher Education*. San Francisco: Jossey-Bass, 1968.
12. Ferster, C. B., and B. F. Skinner. *Schedules of Reinforcement*. New York: Appleton-Century-Crofts, 1957.
13. Fisher, R. A. *Statistical Methods for Research Workers*. Edinburgh: Oliver & Boyd, 1934.
14. ———. *The Design of Experiments*. Edinburgh: Oliver & Boyd, 1935.
15. Freud, A. *The Ego and the Mechanism of Defense*. New York: International Universities Press, 1946.
16. Goebbels, J. *The Goebbels' Diaries 1942–1943* (translated by L. P. Lochner). Garden City, New York: Doubleday & Company, 1948.

17. Guthrie, E. R. *The Psychology of Learning*. New York: Harper & Brothers, 1935.

18. Heidegger, M. *An Introduction to Metaphysics* (translated by R. Manheim). New Haven, Conn.: Yale University Press, 1959.

19. Horney, K. *The Neurotic Personality of Our Time*. New York: W. W. Norton & Company, 1937.

20. Hull, C. L. *Principles of Behavior*. New York: Appleton-Century-Crofts, 1943.

21. Husserl, E. *Ideas: General Introduction to Pure Phenomenology* (translated by W. R. Boyce Gibson). New York: The Macmillan Company, 1952.

22. Jones, E. *The Life and Work of Sigmund Freud*. Vol. 1. New York: Basic Books, 1953.

23. Kant, I. *Critique of Pure Reason* (translated by Norman Kemp Smith). London: Macmillan, 1929.

24. Kardiner, A. *The Individual and His Society*. New York: Columbia University Press, 1939.

25. Krutch, J. W. *The Measure of Man*. New York: Bobbs–Merrill Company, 1954.

26. McClelland, D. "Psychoanalysis and Religious Mysticism" in *The Roots of Consciousness*. New York: D. Van Nostrand Company, 1964.

27. McClelland, D. C., J. W. Atkinson, R. A. Clark, and E. L. Lowell. *The Achievement Motive*. New York: Appleton-Century-Crofts, 1953.

28. McCurdy, H. G. *The Personal World: An Introduction to the Study of Personality*. New York: Harcourt, Brace & World, 1961.

29. Maslow, A. H. *Motivation and Personality*. New York: Harper & Brothers, 1954.

30. Max, L. W. "An Experimental Study of the Motor Theory of Consciousness. I. Critique of Earlier Studies." *Journal of General Psychology*, 1934, Vol. 11, 112–125.

31. May, Rollo. "Existential Bases of Psychotherapy," in *Existential Psychology*, Rollo May (ed.). New York: Random House, 1961.

32. Murray, H. A. *Explorations in Personality*. New York: Oxford University Press, 1938.

33. Osgood, C. E. "The Psychologist in International Affairs." *The American Psychologist*, 1964, Vol. 19, 114–118.

34. Pavlov, I. P. *Conditioned Reflexes*. London: Oxford University Press, 1927.

35. Riesman, D. *The Lonely Crowd*. New Haven, Conn.: Yale University Press, 1950.

36. Rogers, C. R. *Casebook of Non-Directive Counseling*. Boston: Houghton Mifflin Company, 1947.

37. Rousseau, J.-J. *Émile* (translated by B. Foxley). New York: E. P. Dutton, Everyman's Library, 1959.

38. Sanford, N. "Will Psychologists Study Human Problems?" *The American Psychologist*, 1965, Vol. 20, No. 3, 192–202.

39. Schein, E. H. "The Chinese Indoctrination Program of Prisoners of War." *Psychiatry*, 1956, Vol. 19, 149–172.

40. Skinner, B. F. *The Behavior of Organisms*. New York: Appleton-Century-Crofts, 1938.

41. ———. *Walden Two*. New York, The Macmillan Company, 1948.

42. ———. "Are Learning Theories Necessary?" *Psychological Review*, 1950, Vol. 57, 193–216.

43. ———. *Science and Human Behavior*. New York: The Macmillan Company, 1953.

44. ———. "Critique of Psychoanalytic Concepts and Theories." *The Scientific Monthly*, 1954, Vol. 797, 300–305.

45. ———. "Critique of Psychoanalytic Concepts and Theories," in H. Feigel and M. Scriven (eds.), *The Foundations of Science and the Concepts of Psychology and Psychoanalysis*. Minneapolis: University of Minnesota Press, 1956, 77–87.

46. ———. "A Case History in Scientific Method." *The American Psychologist*, 1956, Vol. 11, 221–233.

47. ———. *Verbal Behavior*. New York: Appleton-Century-Crofts, 1957.

48. ———. *Cumulative Record*. New York: Appleton-Century-Crofts, 1959.

49. ———. *The Technology of Teaching*. New York: Appleton-Century-Crofts, 1968.

50. Skinner, B. F., H. C. Solomon, and O. R. Lindsley. "A New Method for the Experimental Analysis of the Behavior of Psychotic Patients." *Journal of Nervous and Mental Diseases*, 1954, Vol. 120, 403–406.

51. Sullivan, H. S. *The Interpersonal Theory of Psychiatry*. New York: W. W. Norton & Company, 1953.

52. Tillich, P. *The Courage to Be.* New Haven, Conn.: Yale University Press, 1952.
53. Wolpe, J. *Psychotherapy by Reciprocal Inhibition.* Stanford, Calif.: Stanford University Press, 1958.

Index